VERNACULAR ARCHITECTURE

VERNACULAR ARCHITECTURE

Henry Glassie

Photographs, Drawings, and Design by the Author

Philadelphia
MATERIAL CULTURE
Bloomington and Indianapolis
INDIANA UNIVERSITY PRESS · 2000

material culture

This is the second in a series of books on material culture, co-published by Material Culture of Philadelphia and the Indiana University Press, edited by George Jevremović, William T. Sumner, and Henry Glassie.

Vernacular Architecture is an expanded revision of the fifth chapter of Henry Glassie's *Material Culture*, published by the Indiana University Press in 1999.

Photographs: cover, Dalarna, Sweden; p. 1, Anadarko, Oklahoma; p. 2, Kütahya, Turkey; p. 3, Somerset, England; p. 7, Lima Parish, Dalarna, Sweden; p. 200, Greene County, Tennessee

Indiana University Press
601 North Morton Street
Bloomington, Indiana 47404-3797 USA

www.indiana.edu/~iupress

Telephone orders 800-842-6796
Fax orders 812-855-7931
Orders by e-mail iuporder@indiana.edu

Material Culture
4700 Wissahickon Ave., Suite 101
Philadelphia, Pennsylvania 19144 USA

www.materialculture.com

Telephone 215-849-8030
Fax 215-849-5535
E-mail info@materialculture.com

The paper used in this publication meets the minimum requirements of American National Standard for Information Sciences — Permanence of Paper for Printed Library Materials, ANSI Z39.48-1984.

Manufactured in China

Library of Congress Cataloging-in-Publication Data
Glassie, Henry H.
Vernacular architecture / Henry Glassie; photographs, drawings, and design by the author.
    p. cm.—(Material culture)
"Expanded revision of the fifth chapter of Henry Glassie's Material culture, published by the Indiana University Press in 1999"—T.p. verso.
Includes bibliographical references and index.
ISBN 0-253-33756-9 (cloth: alk. paper)—ISBN 0-253-21395-9 (pbk.: alk. paper)
1. Vernacular architecture.
2. Vernacular architecture—United States.
I. Title.   II. Material culture (Indiana University, Bloomington)
NA208.G59 2000
720—dc21   00-040679

1 2 3 4 5 05 04 03 02 01 00

CONTENTS

for
James Marston Fitch

VERNACULAR ARCHITECTURE

Glassie. Perthshire, Scotland. 1972

Ahmetler. Çanakkale, Turkey. 1986

Shankharibazar. Dhaka, Bangladesh. 1998

Church. Ferdinand, Indiana. 1969

Mosque. Güre, Edremit, Turkey. 1997

Shinto shrine. Uji, Japan. 1998

Home. Kütahya, Turkey. 1999

Home. Bloomington, Indiana. 1994

Home. County Derry, Northern Ireland. 1972

Home. York County, Pennsylvania. 1968

Home. Hagi, Japan. 1999

Home. Vale, Guernsey, Channel Islands. 1982

Home. Valaiyapatti, Tamil Nadu, India. 1999

Home. Bolat, Konya, Turkey. 1994

VERNACULAR ARCHITECTURE

BUILDINGS, LIKE POEMS and rituals, realize culture. Their designers rationalize their actions differently. Some say they design and build as they do because it is the ancient way of their people and place. Others claim that their practice correctly manifests the universally valid laws of science. But all of them create out of the smallness of their own experience.

All architects are born into architectural environments that condition their notions of beauty and bodily comfort and social propriety. Before they have been burdened with knowledge about architecture, their eyes have seen, their fingers have touched, their minds have inquired into the wholeness of their scenes. They have begun collecting scraps of experience without regard to the segregation of facts by logical class. Released from the hug of pleasure and nurture, they have toddled into space, learning to dwell, to feel at home. Those first acts of occupation deposit a core of connection in the memory.

Were it me, were I the one who would come to build, there would be red clay and pale curls of wood. There would be an orchard outside and shotguns in the hallway. Thick white paint on rough pine boards would connote home and call to mind the soft sounds of dogs and old men on the porch, the cool feel of linoleum on the kitchen floor, the smells of bacon frying. A woman's lilt, an endless melody strung of hymns to Jesus, would wander through it, accompanied by the brisk whisks of a broom.

As we grow, memory runs wild, undirected by future projects. Culture accumulates into an inner resource of association and gathers order aesthetically. This feels good, that bad, while experience widens, memories deepen, and culture complicates through learning.

When the builder's attention is narrowed by training, whether in the dusty shop of a master carpenter or the sleek classroom of a university, past experience is not obliterated. It endures in the strange caves of the brain and in the old habits of the muscles as they seek smooth routes through the air. Education adds a layer. In precept and admonition, in pedagogical technique, if not in content, the teacher brings cultural values into the process of transmission. Students obey or rebel. Inwardly, new ideas mix and coexist with old ones, and the mind, fed by the senses, continues to bounce about, unfettered by consistency. Resolution will come in performance, in dedicated, situated instants of concentration, while planning meets accidents and learning continues.

Despite the rigors of training, the architect remains a full person, at once competent and confused. The building shares in its builder's confusions. It seems right, as a result, because it incorporates the experience that the architect shares — not completely, of course, but completely enough — with those who do not build, but who look at buildings and go into them. The building works because it integrates the tight routines of professional practice with the loose expanse of cultural association. The overtly architectural contrivance covertly absorbs the norms of beauty and social exchange and political order with which the architect, as a member of society, has come to feel at ease.

Architecture is like any realization of potential, like any projection of thought. The things of the world — this sentence, that palace — preceded themselves in the mind as plans. Plans blend memories with a reading of the immediate situation. They are realized in things. They can be reversed in analysis. Things become plans, plans disaggregate into sets of decisions, decisions become intentions. All creations bespeak their creators. They stand before us as images of will and wit. In this, architecture is like other things, and there are no differences among kinds of building. All are cultural creations, orderings of experience, like poems and rituals.

Ağzıkarahan, Turkey. 1982

Vale, Guernsey, Channel Islands. 1982

If every building is a cultural fact, the consequence of a collision between intentions and conditions, if differences of culture and circumstance adequately account for differences among buildings, the question is why we persist in calling some of them vernacular. There are answers.

Few kinds of building have been accorded full study. When we isolate from the world a neglected architectural variety and name it vernacular, we have prepared it for analysis. The term marks the transition from the unknown to the known. The study of vernacular architecture is a way that we expand the record, bit by bit. At work, moving toward a complete view of the builder's art, we bring buildings into scrutiny and toward utility in the comprehensive study of humankind.

Buildings are neglected for different reasons. Some are the exotic products of indigenous people in places unknown to us. But others are familiar, maybe too familiar. The architectural historian who lavishes attention yet again on some canonical monument probably lives in a house of a kind that has wholly eluded serious study. Pondering why some buildings get studied and others do not, we are likely to argue that some buildings are important and others are not. Then pondering the emptiness of that answer, we find that important buildings can be interpreted as displays of the values we value — grandeur, perhaps, or originality — while unimportant buildings display values that we have not yet learned to appreciate. Neglect is a sign of ignorance. The term, I repeat, marks the transition from the unknown to the known: we call buildings "vernacular" because they embody values alien to those cherished in the academy. When we called buildings "folk," the implication was that they countered in commonness and tradition the pretense and progress that dominate simple academic schemes. Folk buildings contained a different virtue. The study of vernacular architecture, through its urge toward the comprehensive, accommodates cultural diversity. It welcomes the neglected into study in order to acknowledge the reality of difference and conflict.

Should we wonder why architectural study has aped the study of art in its erection of a canon of important buildings, we will find, on reflection, a host of causes. One of them has to do with the ease of procedure. Selecting a few buildings, a few architects, and then linking them up chronologically, we can borrow the facile techniques of the historian of great men and events. But taking the comprehensive view and recognizing diversity, the study of vernacular architecture drives toward better historical procedures, ones that focus existentially on action and lead to the construction of a multiplex idea of time. We call buildings vernacular to highlight the cultural and contingent nature of all building.

Proposing distinctions and labeling buildings along the way, the study of vernacular architecture is an approach to the whole of the built world. It favors completeness, recognizes diversity, and seeks ways to use buildings as evidence in order to tell better versions of the human story. In the future, it will be obsolete, but now the term "vernacular" is one of the tools we use when we face architectural objects with a wish to crack them open and learn their meanings.

Materialization

Architecture works in space as history works in time. History interrupts time's ceaseless flow, segmenting and reordering it on behalf of the human need for meaning. Architecture intrudes in the limitless expanse of space, dividing it into useful, comprehensible pieces. Converting space into places through disruption, architecture brings meaning to the spatial dimension.

With astronomy as the extreme instance, the architectural impulse begins in exploration and naming. The baby crawls upon a softness that matures in meaning as time passes and names pile up: the softness is a rug, it is a red rug, it is a mediocre late nineteenth-century eagle Kazak. The explorer ventures into unknown territory to parcel and claim it with names that commemorate his heroism. Through time, names accumulate on the land

and combine to recall its history: the sequence of settlement, the conflict between the invader and the native.

The name is a fleeting means for bringing history into space and marking the land as meaningful. Marking becomes firmer with physical alteration, when a trail is blazed through a forest, or one stone is piled on another to set a limit. More stones confirm the limit and rise into walls: the wall the Chinese built that turned the mounted warriors westward toward Europe, the wall the Romans struck across Britain to cede the heathy highlands to the wild men of the north, the walls of forts along the borders, the walls of prisons and gated communities, the walls of the cottage where the bold thresherman, his day's work done, dandles the baby on his knee.

With the act of physical alteration that calls time into space, implying a past and a future, and with the walls that divide space, at once including and excluding, architecture has happened.

Architecture gives physical form to claims and names, to memories and hopes. As a conceptual activity, architecture is a matter of forming ideas into plans, plans into things that other people can see. Architecture shapes relations between people. It is a kind of communication. The mode of its thinking connects architecture to all of culture, but its mode of realization distinguishes it from other varieties of communication. To be architecture, it must be realized in materials.

The decision to create a building is the decision to destroy some part of the material universe. Things are wrecked — trees are toppled, stone is broken, old houses are razed — to make life better. The desire is for improvement. The process of the desire is technological.

Technology is a corollary of human existence. It is the means of our extension into space, as natural to people as swimming is to fish. As life unfolds, every technological act brings changes in two great relations: the one that always connects the human and nonhuman spheres, the other that is built to connect people with one another.

Framed house
under construction.
Hagi, Japan.
1994

Log house under construction. Lima Parish, Dalarna, Sweden. 1989

Timber, brick, stone.
Halle (Saale),
Germany.
1999

Brick.
King William County,
Virginia.
1978

Stone. Burton Bradstock, Dorset, England. 1972

Architectural Technology

The relation of the human and nonhuman begins its transformation in the first step of technology, the selection of materials. A distinction between local and imported materials was among the first criteria that writers, in England particularly, used to define vernacular architecture. Vernacular buildings are composed of local materials, they argued. During travel, they enjoyed watching the substrate of the earth rise and form into buildings, crossing the land in bands of sandstone, limestone, and granite, and they deplored the rash of red brick buildings that spread along the railways, oblivious to geological differences. Their taste was built on conventional dichotomies: natural and artificial, native and alien, old and new, local and national, handmade and industrial. The contemporary cynic would find their view easy to deconstruct as elitist and dismiss as sentimental. But they were on to something.

During architectural fieldwork, I have taught myself to concentrate on form, but everywhere I go the people whose houses I study classify buildings by materials, and especially by roofing. I found in Turkey that the local historians separated old houses with flat roofs from new houses with pitched roofs covered by purchased materials. In Bangladesh, village people, thinking less about history than social class, divide buildings by the materials of their walls — stuccoed brick versus puddled mud or bamboo lashed in tension — and by their roofs of thatch or tin. In Africa and Latin America, thatch is comparably yielding to tin, and in the rural United States one age gave way to another when wooden shingles were replaced by shiny sheets of metal.

I learned the lesson of this change first in Ireland. In Ballymenone, a farming community where I drew a plan of every house and classified them into four distinct types, the people classified them into two groups by materials, separating houses that were thatched from those that were roofed with slate or metal.

Joe Murphy, Johnny Drumm, and Tommy Love, masters of thatching, taught me the logic that lay beneath their distinction. Thatch makes good insulation. It is warm in the winter, cool in the summer. Environmentally efficient, thatch is also beautiful. Looking downhill at a house he had recently roofed, Tommy Love said, "When it is new with straw, it shines like gold. The sun glints off it, and it is lovely. It is lovely, right enough."

Efficient and beautiful, thatching is also economical. Its main demand is time, and in Ballymenone they say that the man who made time made plenty. Thatch also requires a knowledge of growing things, the understanding of seeds and soil and weather that farmers develop during time passed in place. The material grows from the ground. It is an endlessly renewable resource, and it is processed and applied by hand, with no need for expensive machinery. Thatching takes knowledge and skill, it is a job for the man called handy, but it is a technology that requires no money.

The problem is that thatch demands regular maintenance and frequent replacement. The metal roof obviates the need for constant intervention; it is effectively permanent. The householder is not obliged to be a craftsman or to be connected — as they were in Ballymenone through trades of aid — with neighbors who are skilled. He manages alone without effort or knowledge or talent or social connection. But metal does not suit the climate. It works little better in cool, humid Ireland than it does in hot, humid Bangladesh, where the tin roof roasts you in summer. And metal is not beautiful. Ellen Cutler said it broke her heart when she used the royalties she received from my first book on Ballymenone to strip the thatch from her home and roof it with metal. Her house, she said, had turned ugly. But she made the change because of "the times that are in it."

Those times, in Ellen Cutler's mind, were characterized by the melting away of intimate social orders in the heat of Ulster's political troubles, and they were marked by shifts in fashion. Mrs.

Tommy Love.
Ballymenone.
1973

Joe Murphy.
Ballymenone.
1983

John Gilleece's house, which he thatches himself.
Ballymenone, Fermanagh, Northern Ireland. 1972

Cutler belonged to a small rural community where it was satisfying to live in the largest, loveliest thatched house. Dick, her son, lived in the same place, but he belonged to a vast rural proletariat. He worked for wages paid by an agricultural entrepreneur. She knew he would never move into a thatched house — so old and cranky, so very Irish — so she ruined its looks, turning it ugly to make it suit him. She was successful. When Mrs. Cutler died in 1981, Dick moved his family up the hill, and, as she had hoped, Cutler blood kept flowing on Cutler land. Her change brought continuity.

The metal roof fits the times. The times demand money. Manufactured in a mill beyond the horizon, moved by rail and road, sheet metal roofing obliges people to collect specimens of their national currency. They are drawn into paying jobs, becoming the little wheels in the big machine that gathers wealth for distant capitalists. Out of the house for most of the day and beat at its end, people have no time to build through cordial conversations the friendships that once brought a thatcher to the house in exchange for agricultural produce.

The connections shaped by thatching — between people and nature, between people and people — were direct and intensely local. The change from thatch to tin signals the surrender of local autonomy. In Ireland, as in Bangladesh, people have chosen to adjust to the times. They have chosen permanence, reliance on distant producers, and participation in the international cash economy.

Not from the perspective of a privileged observer, whether cynical or sentimental, but from the perspective of the people who live the life, we can sum things up. In the shift from local to imported materials, there is a loss in environmental efficiency and a loss in beauty. There is a gain in permanence, which is compensation for a loss of skill and social connection. The loss of the pleasure taken from a job well done, and the burden of the need for cash, must be set against the prestige that is supposed to accrue to the one who purchases expensive objects. Become a consumer, one reorients. Breaking away from the neighbors with their delicate sense of local hierarchy, people come into comparison with others who, they say in Ballymenone, have money like hay. What is lost is security. What is gained is the hope that commodities will somehow balance the account.

The meanings that lie in the selection of materials are social and economic as well as environmental. But the environment sets the stakes. Living wisely in a tight place, people learn the environment. They know how to select from it the right materials for the job. The prime virtue in materials is their ability to alter the climate, shaping a little environment within which architecture can be forgotten and life can go on. It is a matter on which cultures differ, but when people seek separation from nature, which all of them do in bad weather, their actions often glide out of the pragmatic and into the aesthetic.

One of the first to write on Irish vernacular architecture, the Swedish ethnologist Åke Campbell, spoke glowingly of the fit of the thatched Irish house to the green Irish land. The house, he said, belonged like a natural feature, blending in like a rock or a tree. To Campbell, to me, and — this is what actually matters — to the people who labor to make the houses look like they do, Irish houses are things of beauty on the landscape. But the goal of their builders is not to have them melt into nature. In brilliant white, the house cracks out of its setting of green and brown and gray. Ellen Cutler told me how they picked the lumps from the bottom of the limekiln and burst them in boiling water to get the whitest, brightest whitewash. A widow in her seventies, Mrs. Cutler whitewashed the walls regularly to hide the natural tones of the stones and to make her house stand proud in the environment. The weather is wet. The lanes are muddy and rutted. Dampness absorbs light into darkness. In Ballymenone, they

County Galway, Ireland. 1972

County Down, Northern Ireland. 1972

describe the world around them as rough and dull. Smooth and bright, its white walls sparkling, the sun glinting off its roof, the house is a victory over conditions.

It is reasonable for the observer in retreat from the artificiality of industrial environments to see something natural in vernacular architecture. It is equally reasonable for people in daily contention with nature to seek its conquest through processes that smooth the rough and brighten the dull, altering the natural into the artificial. Local materials are their resources, their technologies are powered by their own muscles, but their aim is to create emblems of cultural presence. The bright white house claims the land and names it human.

If vernacular technologies involve local materials and the touch of the hand, their contrast is with industrial systems of production. Vernacular technology depends on direct connections: direct access to materials and direct connections among suppliers, producers, and consumers who simultaneously shape landscapes, social orders, and economic arrangements, while wealth circulates in the vicinity. Industrial production employs imported materials and complex machinery. It depends on expansive political powers that maintain the costly infrastructure of transportation and communication, while supporting through law the right of a small minority to amass great reserves of capital.

The distinction is real and important to preserve, for it helps us assure complexity in historical study. While the globe abounds with instances of the shift to industrial production, technologies based on local skills and materials continue, and they are dominant in many of the world's regions. It is important not to lose the distinction in our thinking. And it is important not to exaggerate its clarity. Vernacular and industrial technologies differ in resources and social organization, but they do not necessarily differ in the attitude toward nature.

Industrial production erases nature. In sheets of metal and slick plastic surfaces, there is no memory of natural origins. People must get up and go outside to remember.

Vacationing folks escape to the woods to forget the city, to relax, to get burned by the sun, bitten by bugs, perhaps to find something like a god in nature. Rolling up logs to build a fancy camp, the city sport leaves them round and brown. They still resemble trees, each distinct in the wall and knobby with knots, and he lets them weather to silver to fit his notion of the natural. A part of nature, his vacation home also alludes to history, to the log cabin that stands firmly in the American consciousness as a mythic sign of the time of the beginning. But the log cabin's builder went into the woods to establish civilization.

The wilderness howled around him, sublime and vast and threatening. He chopped into it bravely, felling trees, hewing their faces flat, lifting them into plumb alignment, and trimming their ends flush at the corner. Chinking the gaps between the logs with shingles or rocks, packed with clay and coated with fine lime plaster, he combined natural substances into smooth, true walls. The trees of the forest were attacked, hacked, split, and made to submit to the plan in his head. They were dropped and raised. They were wrenched from the vertical to the horizontal. They were flattened to realize his design in a unified agony of straight lines that sharply marked his disjunction from nature. And then he confirmed his move to artificiality with a consolidating coat of whitewash or a cladding of clapboards. Restorationists tend to strip away these outer layers, leaving the house naked, vulnerable to rot, and creating an image of rusticity to reinforce preconceptions about progress. But the builder intended them from the beginning. Whitewash and clapboarding called up memories of order, of houses in the cities back east, of homes across the water on the tamed landscapes of Ireland and England, and they expressed his hope for improvement. He built to make the world better, to secure a place of control and reason within the mad-

Dovetailed corner-timbering of a log house built on the frontier.
Shenandoah County, Virginia. 1969

ness of the wilderness. A man of culture, he built a farmhouse that stood out of the woods in splendid artifice.

Long before the industrial revolution, technologies had elaborated in the West. The towering oak was brought down and dressed into a timber, straight and square. Then the timber was joined into a frame. If wood was to be the cover, trees were sawed and split into slices, regular in size and shape, that were applied in series to make floors and walls and roofs. Or, clay was dug, soured in a pit, and molded into geometric units that were hardened by fire. Then these interchangeable parts were laid by line into walls. Traditional technologies of framing and masonry included a decisive step — the squared timber, the squared brick — in the process by which nature was erased and the human world was created. The timber embedded in the frame or the brick lost in the wall are not reminders of nature but pieces of plans and proofs of human control.

When the materials were still local and the techniques still manual, the straight timber replaced the bent one and the brick replaced the stone. In its products, industrial technology is less a violation of the vernacular than it is an exaggeration of one desire within the Western vernacular: its intention to set the human being in a role of righteous command.

There is a difference, though, between vernacular technology and its exaggeration by industry. When nature loomed tremendous and people fought back with plows and axes, their actions were heroic. When people sit in temperature-controlled offices and decree the continuation of that ancient struggle, their actions seem heartless. But the fact of continuity remains. It is traditional — folk, vernacular, cultural — for Western designers to treat nature as a resource, a convenient means for realizing the plans that are contrived in the freedom of the head. This attitude is exhibited most clearly in the aesthetic of the artificial, the traditional taste for repetitive, identical units (the bricks of the chimney, the windows of the high-rise apartment building) and for smooth, unified surfaces (the adzed timber and planed plank, the tile of the bathroom and the formica of the kitchen).

Aesthetic continuity eases change. The faces of the thatched roof and the metal roof are smooth and bright when new, both slick as a shaved chin. Plywood and sheetrock, asphalt, aluminum, and vinyl have been welcomed to the American country home as perfections of the old wish for artificiality. Clean, repetitive concrete blocks have been gracefully incorporated into rural building practice on both sides of the Atlantic, replacing clean, repetitive bricks and boards. Folded in an Appalachian cove, the manufactured mobile home stands out of the landscape, a compact, sharp unit, in the manner of its handmade predecessor, the log cabin.

But, despite tradition, experience has been disrupted. Nature conquered nonchalantly at a distance is not like nature conquered face on. The hewn timber and the steel beam both display the aesthetic of artificiality, but the tree I topple and hew to smoothness is my victory. I have known the transformation of nature in my own hands. I am powerful. The steel beam mined and milled by another and buried somewhere in the concrete beneath me is so removed from my experience that it seems to hold no message for my mind. But if I stop to think about it, the message is clear. I am powerless, utterly dependent on a system scaled beyond my control or understanding.

In the struggle for freedom, striving to fulfill our humanity through release from delimiting conditions, we have wriggled out of one trap, only to be caught in another. In pushing against the natural environment, fighting for control and nearly winning, we have deployed weapons — increasingly intricate, expensive, and mysterious machines — that have demanded our surrender to the political and economic forces of a cultural environment. We understand the mechanics of our cultural environment no better than our ancestors understood the mechanics of their natural environment. We have entered a new age of magic and fear.

Technology is more than a handy means for materializing designs. Since technology requires disruptive intervention in the universe, it asks for answers to profound questions. One class of question is cosmological. Whether they are articulated in religious or scientific terms, cosmological answers enunciate first principles, locating people in the world and conditioning their right to create through destruction. In one cosmological formulation, people occupy an enchanted realm. The trees and rocks and the very earth are alive with active force. Performing in a world filled with hungry ghosts and wily demons, people combine prayers and charms with skills and procedures into a technology of appeasement. Their products display respect and awe. In another cosmological tradition, the deities have granted command to humankind, or the people have seized it through cunning or courage. Theirs is a technology of mastery. It yields, by increasing division, products that display the clear separation of culture from nature, and that, like as not, contribute to the proliferation of ecological calamities.

Technology demands answers to cosmological questions and to political questions. While they disfigure nature, people configure orders among themselves, organizing a force for work and structuring relations between those who make alterations in the physical environment and those who benefit from them. Doubly cultural, technology unfolds from theories about the human position in the universe and from theories that govern the distribution of power among people.

Social Orders

Technology's political questions do not come into focus in the situation described as ideal by writers on vernacular architecture. In the ideal, design, construction, and use — domains of potential conflict — unify in a single man who gathers materials from his own land to build for himself the building he wants. Such things happen.

In 1938, Richard Hutto built a barn near Oakman, Alabama. He cut the trees on his own farm, dragged them to the site with a mule, and he raised them, alone, into a building. Its form is what scholars call a double-crib barn, and they can trace the plan from Alabama along the mountains to Pennsylvania, and from Pennsylvania to Central Europe. Mr. Hutto took the form from the memories he developed out of life in his locale. He trimmed the trees, cut them to length, and he notched their ends to interlock at the corner in a variety of timbering that the geographer Fred Kniffen named V-notching. Mr. Hutto called it "roof-topping."

Richard Hutto's barn was all his. It had only him to blame, it seems. But, when we talked in 1964, he attributed its failings to the times in which he worked. He told me he was thinking of tearing it down. It did not satisfy him because he had been forced to build it alone. He did not have the help of a black laborer as Pete Everett did when he built a barn, similar in form and construction, near Pine Hill, Mississippi, one year earlier. Mr. Hutto did it alone, but in the better days of the farther past, he said, a team of neighbors would have gathered to help. With more energy available, the timbers would have been hewn, rather than left in the round. Poles, he called them, not logs. The team would have included experts with the proper tools. The ends of the logs would have been trimmed cleanly with a saw, instead of raggedly with a chopping axe.

Many craftsmen have spoken similarly to me. Enacting the vernacular ideal, they think of themselves as enduring amid decline. When I met Stan Lamprey, a basketmaker in Braunton, a village in Devonshire, England, he was working alone like many American craftsmen, cutting the willows, weaving them into tight baskets, and then selling them to women who used them in shopping and gathering eggs. Stan Lamprey kept making baskets because it was his trade, the source of his pleasure and cash, but he remembered better days, when he worked in Braunton's basket factory. Then the boys did the simple tasks of gathering and preparing the materials, the manager of the factory did the nox-

Logwork.
Corner-timbering of a cabin.
Greene County, Pennsylvania.
1973

Stonework.
Chimney of a log house.
Greene County. 1977

The M. T. Davis farm. Greene County, Pennsylvania. 1973

ious job of commerce, and Stan worked in a sociable place, chatting with his mates, and doing the difficult part of the work that brought him his joy.

When the materials were still local, the skills still manual, the norm in architecture, as in pottery or metalworking or weaving, was not for one person to do everything, from the extraction of materials, through their preparation, to their assembly into usable forms. Work was divided by specialization. Different people filled different roles in a single process, as actors do in a drama, and technology entailed social arrangements.

After more than a decade of rambling fieldwork, during which I came to some understanding of the log buildings of the Appalachian domain, I determined to do it right. With a modest grant, I assembled a team of students — all of them, Howard Marshall, Steve Ohrn, and John Vlach, have gone on to success — and I led them in a survey of the old log buildings of Greene County in southwestern Pennsylvania. It was my best experience as an educator. We learned together in the field.

At work in Greene County, we did not, of course, come to conclusions that would support the idea, so fundamental to the capitalistic mythos, that the frontier was a place of equal opportunity. We found brick mansions as old as the log cabins. In the beginning, there were differences of wealth. The log cabin was more a sign of social class than of rugged individualism. Log buildings did not look like they were made by self-reliant souls who went into the woods with an axe, there to succeed or fail by dint of individual intelligence and industry. Highly consistent in form and technology, the buildings implied a prevalence of collective, rather than individual effort. We did not find competitive individualism at the dawn of American time, but neither did we find the perfect unity of a cultural spirit guiding the hands of the dead. What struck us was how many of the eighty-three buildings we studied could be clustered into small groups, each marked by certain conventions of practice, each signed by a particular master at work within a technological tradition.

John James had not yet published his study of Chartres Cathedral, one of the best of all books on material culture. Examining the great building through exacting measurements, James was able to attribute it, not to a single architect, but to a succession of master masons. Their names are lost, but their peculiarities of technical habit abide in the fabric. Similarly, in details that would become invisible once the building was finished, we discovered builders who had knacks and tricks, particular to them alone. They knew special ways to join sills and frame windows. James named his nameless masons for colors. We named the house carpenters of the frontier after the techniques they used to frame the plate at the top of the wall that received the thrust of the rafters.

In silent wood, the buildings remembered the developed skills of architectural specialists, and, as Warren Roberts has demonstrated, they used a big chest of tools to get the job done. The tools were too many for one man to carry into the wilderness on his back. The builders on the frontier had chopping axes to score the logs, broadaxes to hew them, and saws to make clear cuts. They had augers in different sizes for boring, wedges and froes for splitting, and they had a battery of planes to smooth the boards and edge them with decorative moldings.

A fine, trim house, the log cabin displayed professional practice in its finish and in its most difficult joints. But the rest of the building fluttered with the uncertain touch of the amateur. Though plates and doors were framed consistently and accurately, logs were hewn differently, corner-timbering varied, and there were mistakes in the notches cut to receive the joists. The building — whether a house of one room or an enormous, soaring barn — spoke clearly of a collaboration between a master of the trade and a gathering of willing amateurs.

The collaboration we puzzle out of common old buildings or rare old contracts is easy to understand when we come to places where architecture is not yet dominated by industrial capitalism. Let us shift from architectural speculation to ethnographic certainty, returning to the white houses on the soft green hills of Northern Ireland.

When Paddy McBrien wanted a new home, he went to his neighbor, the mason Tommy Moore, and asked him to build a house on the track of Eamon Corrigan's. Track is the word they use in Ballymenone for plan. The shape of the building is like the track of a cow in the mud that hardens in the sun, leaving an exact sign of her passing. Paddy did not begin with principles, but, like most architects, with historical precedents. Tommy, a professional, the builder of many houses, suggested one change, an additional door to ease the flow of internal traffic. Paddy accepted Tommy's advice, and made another change. Though it would cost him more, he did not want his kitchen to rise inside to the rafters, where soot and cobwebs collect, for that, the old local norm, would make "a rum looking shop." He wanted a neat, flat ceiling, easy to clean, above his kitchen.

Mary McBrien, Paddy's wife, also wanted her kitchen clean. She approved of the ceiling and requested a hallway, a space to divide the inside from the outside, where muddy wellingtons could be left. In the community's old houses, the door — "the hole the mason left" — broke directly into the kitchen, and it was left open to welcome visitors, winds, chickens, and filth. Mary McBrien wanted a separation that would, like Paddy's ceiling, make her kitchen a tidy box. Later, Paddy and Mary would agree that they had made an error. Mary felt her work in the kitchen was lonesome when she could no longer glance out the window and the open front door toward the action along the road. The hallway proved to be a bad thing when wakes were held in the kitchen. You had to upend the coffin and walk it along the twisted route from the kitchen, through the hallway, and out the front door. The body bumping inside the box was not, Paddy said, a sound you liked to hear. But when they built, Paddy and Mary McBrien wanted a modern house, which they designed in their minds by making alterations to an old house that stood in view, across the road and uphill from their own.

Paddy chose the site. It was not on a hilltop, where the old houses stood, but near the road, convenient for vehicles. Tommy and Paddy went to the site and stood in the center of the house, the spot where the hearth would be. They imagined walls around them, then staked them out. It was Paddy's job, then, to cut down trees that grew on his land along the river, to get them home, and square them to become the purlins that would carry the roof across the masonry partitions. His grandfather would have gathered stones. His father would have dug clay and shaped bricks. Paddy made a pile of molded concrete blocks, then Tommy Moore came, and with help from hired laborers and from Paddy himself, he laid the block. The team built the walls, leaving gaps where Tommy marked them. He stood away and located the openings by eye. They look symmetrical in placement, but the measurements I took reveal them to be only roughly so. To finish the job, Tommy subcontracted a carpenter to frame the windows and doors, and to make the furniture, the tables and chairs and dresser of the kitchen.

There Paddy sits, resting with a cup of tea after hard work in the fields. A fire of turf burns on the hearth. The Sacred Heart glows by the door. The house above him is solid proof of his ability to accomplish his dreams. Many minds and many hands conspired, but he was part of the process of design and construction, and now he is free to use the building as he wants. He understands the object he lives in completely, and it teaches him convincingly about the extent and limits of his power in the world. There are things he can do, things he cannot do, but from collaborative creation, he understands about both.

During architectural action, abilities are separated and combined in many ways. When the people of Karagömlek, a village in western Turkey, had collected enough cash from the sale of their carpets to build a new mosque, they hired a master. He was not a member of the community. He came, did his job, got his pay, and left. The master planned the building on the ground, orienting it correctly toward Mecca, and he did the woodwork, framing the window, the

The view uphill, across Paddy McBrien's fields.
Ballymenone, County Fermanagh, Northern Ireland. 1983

The home of Paddy and Mary McBrien.
Ballymenone, Fermanagh, Northern Ireland. 1972

The new mosque. Karagömlek. 1986

Mehmet Öztürk at the gate of his new mosque.
Karagömlek, Çanakkale, Turkey. 1994

door, and the roof, and making the stepped *minber* inside where the *hoca* delivers the sermon on Fridays. My friend Mehmet Öztürk and his neighbors took time away from farming; they gathered and raised the masonry walls. The money won from international commerce, from the sale of their beautiful new carpets, was used to tighten the communal bonds of those who work together at the loom and in the fields, who build together, and who worship together in their own bright white mosque.

Prospering, as an energetic merchant can on the pervious, dangerous border between Pakistan and Afghanistan, Attollah decided to make a gift to his community, a village on the outskirts of Peshawar. A new mosque would bring him prestige, while affirming his intention to belong to the community that differences in riches can disturb so easily.

Attollah hired a young master named Fazul. They drew up no plan. A need for plans seems natural to the architectural historian, but we should not be surprised when we find none. Plans drawn on paper are indications of cultural distance. The amount of detail on a plan is an exact measure of the differences that separate those who conjoin in a building project. The more minimal the plan, the more completely the architectural idea abides in the separate minds of the client and the architect. For Attollah and Fazul, a few words were enough. They both knew what mosques looked like. All Fazul needed to know was the size of the budget. Then he staked out the plan. His laborers dug up the soil, shaped it into adobe bricks, and the building went up. Attollah, pleased with the result, proud of his generosity, joins his neighbors for prayer in the cool interior of the new village mosque.

It is like that on the other side of the Indian subcontinent, when the executive committee of a Hindu temple comes to the sculptor Haripada Pal in Dhaka city. There are no plans and few words. They name a deity. They state a sum. The rest is entirely up to Haripada. He prays and crafts the clay image that is installed in the temple. There he and his patrons join with all the members of the Hindu community to receive through prayer the blessings of God. In communal action, personal differences are not suppressed. They are exploited for the common good. The patron's ability to pay connects with the artist's ability to create, and everyone in the community benefits as differences intermesh in a new unity.

In describing buildings as the creations of their occupants, writers on vernacular architecture choose a simple and concrete way to speak of unity. Design, construction, and use come to oneness in a single mind. In one mind, there is room aplenty for conflict, and the possibilities for conflict proliferate when the designer, the builder, and the user are different people. And when they are, social organization is necessary, and social organizations are apt to shape in conformity with the political orders prevalent in society.

Division in labor is normal in complex architectural technologies. Real complications bring differences among the workers and between the producers who can make things and the consumers who cannot make things. But difference coincides easily with unity when designers, builders, and users connect in culture. The idea of cultural unity is the point behind the scholarly creation of the ideal of the builder-occupant. What makes vernacular architecture is not an occupant who builds but a cultural congruity among design, construction, and use.

When different people share in culture, in basic assumptions about what is right and what is wrong, about what a building should be, when they are of like mind about things, their social arrangements can be built on a political order that is simultaneously hierarchical and collaborative. During interaction, people are assigned roles — in one moment obliged to follow, in another obliged to lead. While the walls of his house are rising, Paddy McBrien is one of the crew, a follower. But when the storm clouds gather and the hay lies on the spread, Paddy, renowned as an agricultural expert, steps into the lead. His neighbors submit to his direction and form a single force. In the fields, Paddy's neighbor Peter Flanagan, an impoverished farm laborer, is one of the hands. At night, courtly Peter Flanagan opens his fiddle case and takes command. Successful farmers and professional masons assemble into a respectful audience for his performance. On the basis of neighborly reciprocity and cooperation, they build unity out of difference.

In the beginning, there was difference. Again we can say that the industrial process is a hyperbolic extension of one feature in the old tradition, in this case its rational division of labor for efficiency in production. Again we can say that, despite continuity, there is a disruption in experience. Cultural unity — congruence in design, construction, and use — does not depend on connections made face to face. The objects of material culture are suited to long-range communication. Carried by trade over great stretches of space, now as always, artifacts can inspire cultural connections between people at a distance. An industrial product, designed by one person and manufactured by many laborers in a big building, can perfectly satisfy the desire of an unknown consumer. It is possible. The designer and consumer might be one in culture. But when hierarchical arrangements expand, unchecked by direct collaborative interaction, then they can harden into a politics of dominance and submission.

Then designers, divorced from consumers, plan houses that they would be unwilling to occupy themselves, and that do not fit the needs of their users. We have the disaster of public housing projects. Then managers, lacking intimate knowledge of the work that must be done, demand the impossible and arrange procedures in strict bureaucratic fashion, leaving little room for the workers to uphold their own standards, or find satisfaction in their daily labor by bringing projects to completion. We have workers who trade their lives for wages, waiting for the unfulfillment of weekends and vacations. Then consumers are reduced to choosing from a set of things, no one of which meets their needs. We have consumers with no option but to purchase commodities that bring them no real joy. As direct social connections disassemble, hierarchical political orders solidify, and malaise shapes into apathy, vague rage, and small fears in search of causes.

With industrial production, a traditional wish for separation from nature, and a traditional pattern of division in work, both extend from order to alienation. In relations between the human and nonhuman spheres, alienation brings bodily comfort. Separated clearly from nature, freed from environmental constraints, cooled when it is hot, heated when it is cold, people feel comfortable. In the relations among people, alienation hastens the pursuit of wealth. Unlimited by obligations owed to other people, no longer locked into a community built on reciprocity and collaboration, people are free to get rich. In the change to alienation, the gain is comfort for many, great wealth for a few.

The loss is more difficult to tally. We have to strain to see the reality of the alternative through curtains of rhetoric, some dropped by the nostalgic, more by the apologists for capitalism.

The old life was simple, we are told. Absurd. Life was anything but simple when people in small groups, interrupted by storms and epidemics and marching armies, managed to raise their own food, make their own clothing, and build their own shelter, while creating their own music, literature, art, science, and philosophy.

It is less fatuous to speak of homogeneity. When I ask people in Turkish villages how they organize work at the loom or in the fields, how they control the flow of water, how they collect to build their own mosques, they answer that they have *birlik*, unity. But their unity is an ideology designed to embrace multiplicity. From living with them, I know they are not homogeneous, if homogeneous means lacking in individuality. Everywhere I go, I find the same range of personality. In the agricultural communities of the mountains of Turkey, the hills of Ireland, or the delta of Bengal, the people are as diverse in psychological makeup, as various in private opinion, as my colleagues in the university. What they have, that my colleagues have in only a diminished version, is a theory of unity. That theory, held in separate minds, draws people into constant engagement.

Engagement — a fit contrast to alienation — puts us on the right track. The great poet W. B. Yeats was close when he said that country people, living hard up against life, have their minds ground sharp. Wisdom is too strong a word, but living in connection, engaged on the one hand with nature, engaged on the other with the neighbors, people know what they know. Their knowledge does not bob on the surface. It sinks and melts into the wholeness of their experience. They might be ignorant about distant matters, but they know who they are. Identity is not a hot topic among them.

Finding the rhythm of the universe during common work, they have learned how to make the land yield fuel and food, fibers to spin, and straw to cover the roof. At work with others, they have created their landscape of trim hedges, neat fields, and white houses on the hilltop. They have built the world they inhabit. In action, in engagement, they have learned from the environment about nature, and from the neighbors about human nature. They have learned what is possible and what is not, and they know they are capable. They know how to set priorities and act decisively. I am talking about the people called peasants. They know how, as individuals, they fit in the world. That knowing leads them to wisdom about as often as freedom leads people to great riches in another place. What they do not have is comfort and wealth. What they do have is confidence.

In Ballymenone, they speak of confidence in terms of faith and trust. You know the local environment, and you have faith that God will provide. He does. Hugh Nolan said he remembered no year so bad that the farmers, working diligently, failed to make their crop, the source of their food and cash. In this place, even in the time of the Famine, in the bad old days of rotten spuds and greedy landlords, the people endured. They found wild herbs on the mountainside, fish in the river. Faith and trust. You can trust people to act properly when they come through

Paddy McBrien's house. Ballymenone. 1972

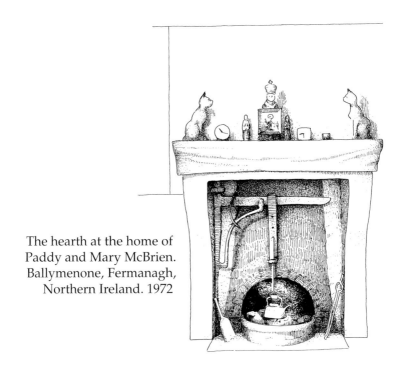

The hearth at the home of
Paddy and Mary McBrien.
Ballymenone, Fermanagh,
Northern Ireland. 1972

the open door of your home. You can trust them to help in times of need. With you, they hold to a neighborly ethic, realized in little acts of reciprocity and cooperation, and founded upon our Lord's commandment to love your neighbor as yourself. In fact, they do not even like one another as particular individuals in particular moments. Differences of personality beget a plenitude of insults, fistfights, and lawsuits. Love is a sacred ideology, the foundation of the social system of trust. In bad times, when troubles strike, the neighbors assemble, someone takes the lead, and the crop is saved, the burned house is rebuilt, the lonely old man is fed.

Paddy McBrien sits in his house. He is a man of power. He knows exactly how his house was planned and built. It protects him adequately from the weather and provides a warm stage for social play. The neighbors round about know exactly who Paddy is. If he falls, they will lift him.

Secure in faith and trust, engaged with the environment, engaged with the neighbors, restricted in freedom, people are confident. They are not very comfortable, they are not rich at all. But they are not bent by the breeze of every fashion, disoriented by every change, frightened by every little noise. They are not lost in quiet desperation with only commodities to use in the struggle to construct a self.

Composition

We began with walls. It would have been as logical to start at the hearth. But I thought of the endless expanse of space, divided it with walls, and then wrote about what it takes to build them, how natural resources are processed and labor is organized. Had I begun at the hearth, where natural resources are transformed by fire into food, I would have made a beginning at the sociable center of life. Then imagining walls around us, just as Paddy McBrien and Tommy Moore did when they stood in the grass and planned Paddy's house, I would have concentrated, not on the walls themselves, on the materials of their building, but on the way they create divisions. Having two sides, walls work to include and exclude. Simultaneously, they make interiors and exteriors.

Architecture divides space for differential experience. It provides an exterior to see and an interior to use. One problem the designer must solve is how to make the exterior and the interior, appearance and function, fit together in a composition.

Though they mix in many buildings, there are two distinct approaches to composing a relation between the interior and the exterior. In one, a geometric figure provides the base for a unified envelope. Internal subdivisions, the conventions of use within, do not register on the exterior. The tipi of the Great Plains and the yurt of Central Asia are circular on plan, one shaped as a cone, the other as a hemisphere. Their geometric exteriors cover, rather than expose, the actions patterned internally around a central fire. In another approach to design, the exterior is the consequence of the life inside.

Standing in the gap between the medieval and the modern, the Wealden house of southern England displays its internal arrangements to a viewer from afar. Where there is a second story, it jetties forward, making its presence known. Windows, different in size and glazing, separate the rooms where people sit from the storerooms where agricultural wealth is kept. From the relation between the offset entry and the lofty hall in the middle, visitors are able to predict accurately the route they will travel from the wet, windy world to the warm place of rest and social exchange. The Wealden house stood as a proud monument to prosperity, and yet it remained generously accessible. It fit its transitional moment in history by belonging at once to the family and the community.

Looking ahead in time from the Wealden house, we will watch the jetties retract into smooth walls. The windows will settle on a single size and space themselves evenly. The door will shift to dead center. The new English house will become a geometric

Wealden house of the fifteenth century.
Weald and Downland Museum. Singleton, Sussex. 1979

Early modern house.
Cressing, Essex, England. 1973

St. Andrew's.
Nether Wallop,
Hampshire,
England.
1972

Illtyd and Rhidian.
Llanrhidian,
Glamorgan,
Wales. 1972

Rood screen. Holy Trinity.
Long Sutton, Somerset, England. 1978

unit that hides its internal operations. Pride will continue, but acts of entry will be interrupted. Visitors will no longer know where they will go or what they will find, once the door is opened and they are ushered along a passage through partitions.

Looking backward, we can see that the Wealden house was designed on the model of the parish church. Stepping down from the tower on the west, to the commodious nave, to the lower chancel on the east, the parish church assembled forms around uses. Its internal volumes expanded to shape its external appearance. The walls enclosed liturgical action. A door on the side, offset toward the rear of the nave and announced by a porch, tells you that you will enter, turn, and then proceed toward the rood screen that divides the nave from the sacred place of the priest. In like manner, you enter the Wealden house, turn, then walk toward the warm place of the master, the priest of the hearth. Behind him, a wall separates the hall where you are welcome from the private apartments reserved for the family. The Wealden house borrows authority from the church. Like the church, it builds form out of use, inviting people in, channeling their motion, then blocking them with a wall that breaks the interior into accessible and inaccessible domains.

Where space breaks internally, the community comes to oneness. In their church, the people assemble before the rood screen, taking communion, drinking the wine that is the blood, eating the wafer that is the flesh, creating among themselves the mystic body of the church. In the house, at exactly the same point in the plan, people sit together, drinking and eating, forming friendships and ratifying the sacred order of their community.

We call buildings like the Wealden house vernacular to give them distance, to prevent ourselves from casually using our own cultural assumptions during interpretations of buildings created by other people. In the study of vernacular architecture, one assumption we must dispense with is the familiar dichotomy of the public and private. Modern law makes clear distinctions between the public and the private, between kinds of real estate that individuals can and cannot alienate by sale, between places of access and places of trespass. People in rural communities construct a realm of rights between the public and the private. They shape a middle zone on the landscape where members of the community have rights of way and permission to exploit collective resources, picking windfalls in the forest, grazing herds on the commons. An understanding of architecture requires, at least, a recognition of the central realm of communal space, lying between private space and public. The nave of the parish church and the hall of the Wealden house were not precisely public or private. They were communal. Open to the community, they were not like the highway that was open to everyone, nor were they like the chancel of the church or the bedroom of the house that were open to only a select few.

The scene can be imagined: men and women, different in station, coming and going, mingling freely in the big smoky hall. In the grand old ballads, the hall was a place for feasts and murders. But exactly how the Wealden house was used is a matter, at last, of conjecture. There is no need to guess about the houses of Ballymenone.

Ballymenone's most common house is not common in Ireland. It is historically akin to the Wealden house, the result of English settlement after the failure of the rebellion of Ulster's chiefs at the end of the sixteenth century. The Wealden house and the old house of Ballymenone are similar in form. Both are centered by an open space rising to the rafters. A hall in England, it is called a kitchen in Ireland. Ballymenone's kitchen is flanked by rooms, a parlor on one side, a bedroom and a pantry on the other. These rooms are private spaces, closed during the day, and entered only by invitation. But the offset front door is open to everyone who walks across the fields. It is bad manners to knock, worse manners to stop guests at the door. They enter, walk across the kitchen floor, and sit down by the fire, receiving hot tea and joining conversations that were going before they came, that will continue after they have gone. The space flowing from the hearth

Peter Flanagan's house.
Ballymenone, County Fermanagh, Northern Ireland. 1973

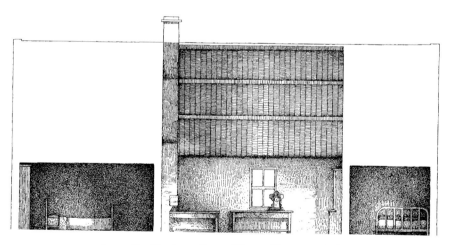

Longitudinal section of Peter Flanagan's house.

and through the front door, running from fire to fire on the hill-sides, expanding through the fields and down to the bog where people have the right to cut turf for fuel and raise vegetables — all that space is not private. People cross it and use it within customary limitations. It is not private, nor is it public. Public space is restricted to the narrow tracks of the roads that cut through the countryside, carrying people who do not know the local etiquette and who, therefore, cannot enter communal space properly.

Communal space opens between the public and the private. As in the cognate houses of Ballymenone, as in the church of the parish, space in the Wealden house probably did not divide into public and private at the front door. The house, instead, divided the communal from the private at the wall beyond the high hall.

Not until houses became geometric units did private space and domestic space become coterminous. Even then the discrimination is not fine enough. The partitioned interior of the geometric unit contained working spaces to the rear that were entered casually, convivial spaces to the front that were entered formally, and procreational spaces that visitors entered at the risk of their lives. Access was different to the kitchen, the parlor, and the bedroom. Unifying those spaces with the name private thwarts rather than advances architectural analysis. In the house of my boyhood and in the house where I live today, the neighbors come through the back door and into the kitchen without knocking. People I do not know come to the front door and wait. If they get in, they go where I take them, probably to the kitchen. The bedrooms are for the family. The exception is my daughter's room, which, being her house, often fills with her friends, who burn incense and listen to old-time rock and roll. This is to speak only of the house. Around it run outer rings, porches and yards, that segment space still more. The simple duality of private and public suffices for lawyers, but it is not complex enough or subtle enough to organize architectural study. The public and the private lie at the opposite ends of a wide spectrum of distinct spatial experiences.

Displaying its interior upon its exterior, the old Wealden house extended a communal welcome, and then divided space internally. It was like the parish church, and it differed from later houses in the way that the parish church, a building for the community, differed in its day from the great cathedral. A truly public building, the cathedral presented an imposing, geometrically composed facade. Like the human face, the facade was bilaterally symmetrical. The unity of two parts was also tripartite: like the triumphal arches of Rome, a tall door was flanked by lower doors, all offering points of beginning for motion toward the triumph over death represented by the cross.

In England's domestic architecture, the aim of composition shifted. The old house had no facade. Its exterior was the consequence of its interior. Its interior was the result of patterns of use. Patterns of use brought communal and familial orders into interaction. The new house was simpler. It had a facade. A regular arrangement of regular openings, the facade obstructed entry, obliterating communal space in a wall that divided public space from an assembly of domestic places. To the public, the new house offered, like the cathedral, a mask of grandeur, figured in bilateral symmetry.

England's change in domestic architecture, accomplished between the sixteenth and eighteenth centuries, was a shift from organic design, in which the exterior is the skin of the inside, to geometric design, in which the outside masks the interior behind a facade. The facade, a smooth surface punctured by repetitive openings, displays the aesthetic of artificiality. Like an industrial product, it hides rather than exposing the processes that lie behind it. But the geometric facade came long before industrialization, just as geometrically contrived building materials did. These smooth, repetitive things — the symmetrical facade, the squared timber and the squared brick — manifest the desire for order that drove the development of industrial procedures.

Walls separate insides from outsides. Buildings link insides with outsides. One linkage is created through the massing of

Ellen Cutler. Ballymenone. 1976

volumes, perhaps organically, perhaps geometrically, and often in a combination of these approaches to composition. Another connection is made through ornament.

Architectural Decoration

Ornament creates an exciting tension within architectural experience when the inside and outside are treated differently. Ellen Cutler whitewashes the exterior of her house in Ballymenone. The whitewash confirms the unity of the building and separates it cleanly from its natural surround of muddy lanes and grassy fields. On its exterior, her house is solid and singular, artful in its massing and its unrelieved whiteness. Step over the threshold. The brightness of the whitewash continues in the buffed and polished surfaces of the things she calls ornaments: the brass candlesticks and enameled dogs on the mantel, the pictures and plates on the walls. But similarities are swept away by differences. The hard, plain unity of the exterior yields to the softness of textiles, to a busy, glittery dance of little things, to a rainbow of color and a happy cacophony of pattern.

The walls of her kitchen darken from smoke nearly as often as the walls outside darken in the wet weather. Nearly as often as she whitewashes the exterior, she papers the kitchen, covering its walls with running, repetitive patterns of medallions. Mud tracked in by the damned old men, when they come from the fields for their tea, causes her to scrub the floor every day. So it will shine, she covers the floor with a smooth sheet of linoleum that brings another pattern to her kitchen. And more patterns come on the strips of cloth that cover the tables, curtain the openings, and run along the shelves of the mantel and dresser.

Mrs. Cutler painted the fireplace green with big red dots, like the berries on the holly at Christmas. On the dresser, built into the wall across from the hearth, she arranges plates so they will sparkle or glimmer or glow with the mood of the fire. She calls the dresser's plates "delph." Her plates were manufactured in

Ellen Cutler's dresser.
Ballymenone.
1977

Ellen Cutler's house.
Ballymenone, Fermanagh, Northern Ireland. 1972

England and Ireland, but her name recalls the city in Holland where beautiful blue-and-white plates were made in the seventeenth and eighteenth centuries, and then exported to England and England's colonies to be put on domestic display. Ellen Cutler defines delph as "not for using." The plates for the day's meals are hidden out of sight. The ones displayed on the dresser are washed often and lovingly. It makes her, she says, "happy as money" to wash them, bathing them like babies in a basin, and setting them up in neat gleaming rows on the shelves of her dresser.

Each of the plates on the dresser was a gift from a neighbor, a friend, a member of her family. Like friendships, plates last forever with care and break in one careless moment. Plates make apt gifts, and assembled on her dresser, her plates are her friends. Her social network could be accurately reconstructed from a list of the people who gave her the plates that she loves enough to display on the dresser and wash once a week.

Smoke from the hearth swiftly films the plates with dullness. Always gleaming and clean, the delph of her dresser is the private collection and art exhibition of a "house-proud" woman. Luminosity is the primary intent of her aesthetic, and her plates shine in bright counterpoint to the necessary mess of a workaday farmhouse. The plates reflect light through her kitchen, and they add to its lively mix of color and pattern. White and green and cobalt blue, the plates carry transfer-printed pictures. Like the plates displayed on the walls of a Turkish home, the plates on Ellen Cutler's dresser were inspired by Chinese porcelain. Things to see, not things to use in eating, they carry, like Turkish plates, pictures of things not eaten. They do not show wheat and sheep, but flowers and birds, the lovely ornaments of nature that Mrs. Cutler calls God's messengers.

The difference between the outside and inside is as sharp in the home of İsmail and Narin Yıldız in the magnificent village of Gökyurt in central Anatolia. The exterior is a massive expanse of stone, pierced by small windows. A large door swings to admit you to the runway through the middle of the house, a frank place for agricultural work. At Mrs. Cutler's, the cattle live in a byre built onto the end of the house. Here the cattle live on the floor below. On this, the top level of the Yıldız home, useful pots and baskets are lined into neat rows, and small doors open through the thick walls. You step out of your shoes, over the threshold, and into the interior. The floor spreads with soft, piled carpets, rich in color and pattern. Cloth in bright floral patterns covers the soft cushions on the floor and on the inbuilt seats along the walls. A shelf carries tinned copper bowls and enameled plates around the room near the ceiling. Like the delph on Ellen Cutler's dresser, the silvery vessels, a row of little moons, receive and transmit the light from the fire dancing on the hearth.

In Mrs. Cutler's lovely whitewashed and thatched house, one framed picture on the wall shows a lovely whitewashed and thatched house. Stretched in another frame, a piece of cloth is embroidered "Lead Me and Guide Me." In the Yıldız home, the framed pictures bear glittery calligraphed inscriptions of Koranic texts. The only book in Mrs. Cutler's kitchen, her Bible, rests on the windowsill. The only book in the Yıldız home, the Holy Koran, hangs in an embroidered bag on a wall by the fireplace. In both houses, pots full of flowers stand in the light in the windows, welcoming natural beauty to the interior.

What is true of these two houses, one in Ireland, one in Turkey, is true generally of farmhouses in Ireland and Turkey, and what is true at the western limits of Europe and Asia is true, too, of many places in North America, both rural and urban. In northern New England and the Maritime Provinces, on the farms of the Southern Mountains and the ranches of the West, among Hispanic and Native American people in the Southwest, the French in Louisiana and Quebec, African Americans in the South, and Irish Americans in the big cities of the Northeast, the house is often austere without and ornamented within, at once hard and soft, plain and fancy, restrained and expressive.

The Yıldız house.
Gökyurt.
1987

Gökyurt. Konya, Turkey. 1987

The house presents a hard, clean, undecorated exterior to see and a cozy, ornamented interior to use. In its elevation, the house unfolds from a logic of engineering and makes an appeal to the intellect. As a device for communication, the exterior unites the viewer and the occupant in rationality. Internally, the house comforts the body and delights the senses. It provides soft seats and a titillating array of textures, patterns, and colors. The weary bones find rest, the eye finds excitement. As a device for communication, unfolding from the householder's interests and taste, the interior stimulates engagement. Mrs. Cutler and Mrs. Yıldız make tea at the hearth. The tea does what the room does. It restores and pleases the guest. Ellen Cutler and Narin Yıldız serve the tea, and then sit with their guests in talk. The talk does what the tea does. It makes friendships possible.

During the study of traditions in which men are the builders of walls, students are often frustrated in the search for the contribution made to architecture by the half of society who are women. In discovering a few women who design and build — like the earnest woman William Morris put to work as a stone mason in his utopian novel *News from Nowhere* — scholars are distracted from the solution to their problem. The problem is an inadequate definition of architecture. If buildings are distinct among the things of material culture precisely because they have both interiors and exteriors, and if buildings are the creations of their creators, then the search for women in architecture should not baffle us.

Divisions in labor are apt to clarify in line with other divisions made in society. Architectural practice is split by gender as well as by class and age and political power. There are traditions in which women do the building. Women dominated architecture in central North America before the European conquest. Africa offers numerous instances of women who build and of women and men who build together. But in many places, men build the house and women build the home within it.

The problem, as I said, lies in the definition. The prevalence of men in the record indicates that architecture has been reduced to a matter of building the walls and arranging the look of the elevation. The exterior is crucial to the serious work of sheltering people from the climate and proposing an image of civil order. The interior is crucial to the serious work of raising families and building communities through intimate exchange. The lack of interest in interiors is part of an art-historical orientation to architecture as a sort of sculpture that can be adequately represented by slides of elevations projected in dark classrooms. Teaching becomes easy and contributes to a gross simplification of the architectural reality. The house is reduced to a shelter and a sign of status and public order that can be accommodated easily by histories that serve economic and political interests. If the intimate ordering of common life mattered in history as much as it does in reality, then the interior would matter, families would matter, communities would matter, and women would be in the story. Architecture would be defined correctly, and buildings would assume the powerful role they deserve in history.

One real problem cannot be avoided. Houses are enclosures for domestic environments. When men build the walls and women arrange the space within, what men create is likely to outlast what women create. The textiles spread on the floor and the crockery arrayed on the dresser are easily swept away by time. When Dick Cutler moved his family into Ellen Cutler's house after her death, her dresser of delph displayed to him, as it had to her, communal connections and an old-fashioned taste. The difference was that he hated what she loved. He took an axe, smashed the china to bits, and threw it out in the street. James Deetz has discovered the residue of such violence in archaeological sites in North America and South Africa. But potsherds cannot be reassembled into an understanding as rich as the one Mrs. Cutler gave me when we sat at her hearth and chatted. The walls of her house survive. But her interior has been replaced by another. It is gone.

After the people are gone, and the old house stands empty, stripped of its possessions, it offers better information about its

Facade of the Sri Minakshi Sundaresvara Temple.
Madurai, Tamil Nadu, South India. 1999

male creators than it does about its female creators. Maybe the name of a woman as well as a man can be teased out of the documents, but her contribution is more transient than his. The solution is to switch from archaeology to ethnography, leaving the empty Wealden house and entering the house of Ballymenone, stepping through the doorway, turning past the dresser of delph, and coming to the glowing hearth where women and men collaborate in hospitality.

Ethnographic study builds in our understanding a sturdy alternative to familiar experience. It ought to enhance our capacity for historical guesswork. Surely, it will lead us to a more comprehensive definition of architecture. That definition will, at the least, alert us to what we cannot know when all we have to study is an empty house in ruins.

We are luckier in the study of old buildings when the ornamental urge of the interior fuses permanently in architectural fabric and spills through the openings to appear on the exterior. Ornament can turn the building inside-out by making the facade into an exhibition of painting and sculpture, as it does in the houses of Nubia and the temples of South India. Much more frequently, external ornament is restrained by the Ruskinian ideal. It reinforces the massing, and provides a foretaste of the delights inside, by clustering at the entry, running around the windows, and marking the edges of the form, its conjunctions of different planes.

When the building's exterior exhibits two aesthetics, one of massing and one of ornament, it speaks at once of two needs. Those needs cut different tracks through time, doubling the building's utility as historical evidence. In its basic massing of tower, nave, and chancel, the English parish church remained stable for centuries. At the same time, the shapes of doors and windows, and the types of ornament that ran along the eaves, climbed the tower, and filled the interior, changed frequently and quickly in harmony with international ecclesiastical fashion.

The form of the parish church remained stable because it was designed to meet the needs of people at worship, and those needs did not change. The congregation needed to connect to God and to one another. The form of the church was right for the work. Details did change because people wanted the church of their parish to symbolize their collective success. They banked extra wealth into a communal building that marked their progress. The church changed to fulfill their need for pride. In meeting two needs at once — building and symbolizing community — their church simultaneously displayed patterns of continuity and patterns of change.

Complexity in Architectural Time

Temporal mixing characterizes the buildings called vernacular. The English parish church, a world wonder of architectural creativity, carries the vernacular idea deeply into time. If vernacular buildings tick with many clocks, changing different components at different rates to display continuity and change at once, then they contrast with buildings that belong perfectly to one moment in time. Nonvernacular buildings are wholly original, new in every detail. Here we have come prematurely to an important conclusion. No building is entirely new. If it were, it would be utterly incomprehensible. Rejecting every old convention, lacking windows and doors, serving no function of shelter or social division, the thing might be sculpture, but it would not be a building. No matter how grandiose or revolutionary the creation, there must be some tradition, some presence of the common and continuous — of the qualities called "folk"— or people would not be able to understand it or use it. In their mixing of the old and the new, all buildings are vernacular, the products of real people in real situations. But within practice, attitudes differ.

In the nineteenth century, American designers created houses that were intended to be different from the common run — dif-

ferent and better. The designers offered their plans through publications to people who wanted houses that would signal their
estate and separate them from their neighbors. The house was
new, but look at its plan, and you will find that the designer did
exactly what Paddy and Mary McBrien did when they wanted a
new house. He took an old house and remodeled it, adding or
subtracting doors and partitions.

It will come as a surprise to you, but there are still historians
who think society is layered like a cake, with a few leaders at the
top and many followers below. They make the job of history easy
by treating the written record as the wellspring of ideas that
trickle down to the masses. But, with regard to architectural form
and order, the nineteenth-century publication was not a source
for novelty so much as it was a mechanism for recycling. It was
a new cog in the ongoing apparatus of vernacular design. The
new plan in the new book would not have seemed wholly alien
to the builder and his client because it was adapted out of the
cultural experience they shared with the designer. The plan they
found in print, then, was easy to modify, normally by simplify-
ing it in the direction of houses they already knew — houses like
those from which the designer lifted his inspiration. Repeatedly,
nineteenth-century books offered tricky versions of eighteenth-
century plans. The builder's source might be the book, but the
book's source was the builder's old tradition.

In most localities in the United States, we find a few nineteenth-century houses built right out of the book by insecure rich
people who chose to align themselves with unknown others. In
the same places, we find many nineteenth-century houses that
combined new ideas out of books with old ideas from the vicinity. At once fashionable and familiar, those houses conspicuously
mixed change with continuity.

The Yankee builder was not daunted by the arrival of a novel
form in the earlier nineteenth century. The new Greek Revival
house was a little temple with a portico; it positioned a gabled

block symmetrically between flanking wings. The Yankee builder had two basic arrangements at hand. One of them went back to the seventeenth century in New England, then on to the sixteenth century in southeastern England. It raised a chimney between a hall and a parlor, and placed a kitchen centrally within a run of rooms across the rear. The other, belonging to the eighteenth century, provided a corridor for circulation among the rooms, and set the kitchen in a back wing. The Yankee builder used both of these ideas to make something like a Greek Revival house. In the gabled block, he set the hall and parlor in a line, often running a corridor along the side. Then dispensing with one of the flanking wings as frivolous, he moved the kitchen into the other, increased its size, and gave it a door to the front, so that old friends could come on in. The ornamental door in the main gabled block was for formal entry, and the farther the house moved west, the more likely the builder was to skip it altogether. The Yankee builder's house looked enough like the new house, and it acted enough like the old houses.

The Southern builder did it more easily. He took an eighteenth-century house with rooms on either side of a hallway, then added a gabled portico, a false front of fashion, behind which the house remained unchanged in form and use. Southern builders, like Northern builders, were knotted into the national network of communication that brought them new ideas through publications. But they reacted differently. The difference in the Northern and Southern response reveals a difference in culture that was hardening toward war in the period of the Greek Revival, the 1830s and 1840s. The Southern builder held the national fashion on the porch, like an unwelcome guest. The Northern builder invited it in, reshaping his whole house to suit the times, while preserving the intimate arrangement of space that the people of his place knew how to use.

Nineteenth-century builders merged the old and the new in their houses. The plans in the books that inspired them did quite

Greek Revival house.
Sullivan County,
New York.
1968

Greek Revival house:
the single-wing form.
Otsego County,
New York.
1965

Late, western version of the single-wing house.
Madison, Wisconsin. 1992

Northern Greek Revival: side-hall, temple-form house with wings.
Otsego County, New York. 1968

Southern Greek Revival: I-house with a portico.
Sevier County, Tennessee. 1975

the same thing. They blended the old and the new. A purer novelty lay in the book's ornamental details. Disconnected from direct use, ancillary to the building's internal functioning, decorative details were easy to change. Symbolizing pride in the nineteenth-century house, as in the medieval church, they accomplished their social work by newness. Still, the designer tended to place the ornaments on the houses in his book in accord with traditional practice. They gathered at the openings and ran along the edges of the form, just as in the Middle Ages. The builder borrowed easily from the book, taking new details and popping them into the old spots. It was enough for his house to seem Italianate — up to date in the decades after the Civil War — if he tucked a row of brackets under the eaves and rounded the tops of the windows. A lower pitch to the roof would cap it off correctly. The house was fashionable, new in its detail, but its form was most likely an Italianate revision of the Greek Revival modification of the Georgian house of the eighteenth century.

Since decorative details alone could signify fashion, and since they fit into the composition at conventional points, around openings and along edges, it was not hard for builders to create houses that were fashionable and familiar at once. Old forms were gussied up with flashy ornaments. The nineteenth-century builder's creations tell, then, a simple story, comparable to that of the parish church. It is a story of social continuity and stylish change. The plan held steady while ornaments came and went, and the building displays a hierarchy of value that usefully challenges the simple, progressive narrative of the historian. The building says clearly that social interaction matters more than shifts in fashion, that local orders matter more than national orders. It says that what continues matters more than what changes. A history that tells only a tale of change misses the most important part of history. Its story is trivial.

The hierarchy of value in the English parish church, where the continuity of sacred action was more important than the changes that signaled worldly pride, sets a clear pattern. The pattern, though simple and schematic, captures the reality in America well enough for many regions. But it misses the excitement in the North.

The book was part of the system of vernacular design, and the book was part of the system of industrial capitalism. The plan in the book made architecture into a commodity. Some people simply bought what they were sold, building as they were told. Others bought selectively, choosing bits to arrange into proof of their awareness of fashion. And many played with their new commodities, ordering and reordering them willfully to suit themselves. The Northern landscape is peppered with extravagant confections, but the clearest sign of the new spirit — of the builders' victory over their cultural conditions — lies in the blatant mixing of decorative styles.

The builders' innovative creations are ignored by critics who should be thrilled by their creativity, but who continue to fixate on the rare big house built lazily out of the book, proving that it is not creativity but class prejudice that focuses their study. The builders' creations madden the modern observer charged with the task of classifying buildings by style. Those dead people are supposed to move obediently from Greek to Gothic to Italianate, then on to Queen Anne. What they did, instead, was to bundle influences into a single decorative style for which the best name is the nonspecialist's label of Victorian. They took doorways from the Greek Revival, jigsawed trim and pointy gables from the Gothic, brackets from the Italianate, towers from the Queen Anne, and combined them into a new vocabulary of ornament that they applied in the traditional manner to buildings that broke all the rules, departed from the national sequence, and stood as meaningful symbols of pride in their localities.

Especially after the Civil War in the Deep South and in the westering reach of the North, the builders did not comply. They engaged in exhilarated play with commodities. In their willingness to pick and choose and make ungainly combinations, they

I-houses decorated with a mix of Greek, Gothic,
and Italianate detail. Fincastle, Virginia. 1977

Georgian box with a Greek memory and Queen Anne
aspirations. Bibb County, Georgia. 1975

Gothic gable and Greek Revival doorway.
Wintersport, Maine. 1978

displayed a spirit we claim for ourselves, thinking of it as so peculiar to these late days that we call it postmodern. In fact, that spirit has been with us since the parish churches of the Middle Ages that are marvelous precisely because of their impurity, their energetic accumulations and assemblies. The difference is that the builder in medieval England or Victorian America played with commodities on the surface of a deep and abiding order. Postmodern play takes place in the air above nothing.

Compositional Levels

Now the walls belong to a composition. Acts of composition bring interiors and exteriors together, massing and ornamenting buildings into units that contain diversity. Then composition expands, and meanings complicate, as buildings are set in relation, one to the other in space. While building walls, people perform on a complex field of influence, balancing the natural and the cultural. By weighing the influences of the natural environment against social and economic influences, we will have a way to begin a consideration of the expansive orders of composition.

It is hot on the vast, flat delta of Bengal, so hot that the climate must figure powerfully in architectural planning. At home in the village, cooking takes place outdoors in fair weather. The heat of the fire disperses, and the woman at work gains a touch of relief from the winds that find their way from the river. It is tropically hot, and it is wet. Rain is an insufficient name for the downpours of summer. In the rainy season, the fire for cooking is moved beneath a roof that is pitched steeply to shed the water. The roof is held aloft by impaled posts. Between the posts, bamboo screens make frail walls. Coolness comes in, the heat of the fire escapes.

A source of heat as well as sustenance, the kitchen stands away from the other buildings that comprise the home. Normally the family is a joint one, made up of brothers, their wives and children, and the old father and mother, should they linger in

Kazipara.
Rupshi, Rupganj,
Bangladesh.
1995

Gillande.
Manikganj. 1987

Norpara. Shimulia, Bangladesh. 1996

life. The members of the joint family pool their resources of labor and capital for the common good. The wife of one of the brothers is detailed for kitchen duty, freeing the others for agricultural work.

Each nuclear unit has its own separate building. Like the kitchen, it is entered directly; opening the door brings fresh air to the people inside. Unlike the kitchen, it is often partitioned. It is a private place for sleeping and the keeping of goods. Visiting, like cooking, takes place outside, in the shade beneath the trees. In wet weather, people shift for talk to the verandas that cross the fronts of the buildings.

Every village exhibits a mix of architectural technologies. The walls might be raised of layers of clay or blocks of clay that make a cave of coolness inside. They might be built of impaled posts and bamboo screens that admit stirrings of air. Clay walls melt and bamboo walls break away in the floods that lift slowly over the flat terrain. Walls go, the place remains, and people rebuild on the old site; not every year, if it is the will of God, but once or twice in a lifetime. Fragile constructions employing local materials seem adaptive in the environment, but the people want freedom from conditions. Sturdy brick walls are what they would have if they could afford them, and gathering a little money, they work for permanence. They replace wooden posts with squared concrete beams, sunken in the soil to carry the light walls that are framed on the ground and then raised. Increasingly, the walls and roof are covered with the sheets of corrugated iron that people call tin.

But local materials — clay and wood and thatch — are still the norm. One neighbor builds thick clay walls, another lives behind flimsy screens of twill-woven bamboo. The simultaneity of different techniques shows that no one of them is truly suitable; the climate is extreme.

The unity of planning shows that this is the best that can be done. Whether the family is rich or poor, whether the buildings are large or small, built of bamboo and thatch or concrete and iron, they stand independently. There is a kitchen, there are bedrooms for every couple, and each one is a building with its own walls. The house — the *bari* — is a cluster of houses, open to the sky. Each building is raised above the flood on its own earthen plinth. All are protected from the sun by the trees that grow around them. Every building stands alone to receive every blessing of breeze.

The village home of Bangladesh meets the family's needs for connection and separation, while modifying as well as it can the natural conditions of heat and damp.

For contrast, come to Dalarna in central Sweden, where it is cold and the snow drifts in heaps. The fire for cooking is tucked in a corner. An open hearth in the past, a stove today, it sends heat toward the table where people sit to eat in the opposite corner. Cozy, curtained beds run in a snug row along the back wall, warmed by the fire. Step out of the room, and you are not outside as you would be in Bangladesh. You stand in a chilly lobby. Closing the door behind you, before opening the door to the exterior, you prevent cold air from getting into the house.

The old Swedish house is a unit, compressed around sources of heat. The walls are built of logs, trimmed to ride tightly one upon the other. There are no chinks for winds to sneak through as there are in the log houses of the United States. The walls are solid wood, a fine insulation, and they are thick and airtight. The mass of the building is unified by paint, and it is centered by a narrow, gabled porch. Though Dalarna is famed in the annals of folk art for the vivid decoration of the interior, the porch carries the only decorative detail applied to the exterior. The porch calls attention to the door and provides protection from the weather while the door is opened. Inside in the lobby, there is a choice of three doors: the door on one side leading to a parlor, the door in the middle leading to a bedroom, the door on the other side leading to the room for daily life, where food is cooked and consumed, where people gather for talk by day and sleep at

Tibble.
Leksand. 1991

Tibble.
Leksand, Dalarna,
Sweden. 1989

Fräsgården. Leksboda, Dalarna, Sweden. 1989

night. All of these rooms have fireplaces that together build heat in the middle of the house.

Within its straight, heavy timber walls, the house of Dalarna gathers the kitchen together with different places for sleeping and with formal and informal locations for socializing. Under one roof, it assembles activities that are scattered in the village home of Bangladesh. In both places, the houses exhibit the knowledge that people develop during lives of environmental engagement. Adjusting intelligently to different conditions, the farming people of Bangladesh and central Sweden create houses that exemplify distinctly different formal arrangements — one of dispersal, the other of compression.

Things tend to fly apart or collapse. During composition, the designer must reconcile the contrary pulls of centrifugal and centripetal forces, accommodating both at once in plans that are liable to move in one direction or the other: toward dispersal or toward compression. At the domestic level, where cooking and eating, sleeping and entertaining combine, the designers of Bengal choose dispersal, while the designers of Dalarna choose compression. Environmental understanding is crucial to their decisions. Let us shift now to the next level of complexity in composition, where domestic work connects with work of other kinds.

In Bangladesh, the buildings that are the bedrooms and kitchen of the family stand among others. There are agricultural buildings, sheds to store produce and shelter cattle, and when the village has a craft specialty, there is a workshop for weavers or potters, carpenters or smiths. Screens and verandas make connections, and the buildings shape into a neat square around an open courtyard, with the houses for sleeping in a line along the rear. The shop to the front provides one entry. An offbeat opening at a corner provides another route to the courtyard where work goes on, where food is cooked and pots are made.

Returning to Dalarna, we expect compression and get a little, for the agricultural buildings often run together, but the situation is more similar than different. The house makes one side of a square, the back side as in Bangladesh, and, as in Bangladesh, all doors open into the courtyard. Entry is made through a barn in front or through a gateway on the side.

At this more expansive level of design, planners in Bengal and Dalarna perform similarly. They build the house as part of a larger compositional unit that forms a square around a courtyard. It is not that they have forgotten about the climate. That would be impossible. But arranging buildings primarily for efficiency in work, and not separating domestic work from agricultural and industrial work, they create a courtyard that facilitates circulation among all the buildings. In doing so, they choose a plan that is tight enough for the Swedish farmer, who must work through the cold and snow, and loose enough for the Bengali farmer, who must work through the heat and rain. Their plan, by establishing order through the geometric figure of the square, asserts an ascendancy of the rational over the natural. And their plan, at once open and closed, locates a midpoint between the extremes of compression and dispersal.

The world of architecture contains examples aplenty of more compressed designs. On the pastoral highlands of the British Isles, notably in Devon and Wales, the separate steading was centered by a longhouse. Retreating from the wide, wild world around it, the longhouse was an agricultural fortress, housing the stock at one end and the people at the other, beneath a single roof. Writers from the seventeenth century allow us to picture the Irish house of those days. It was a thatched longhouse, framed of crucks, with walls of mud or wattle and daub. The interior was one space, narrow, lengthy, and unpartitioned, with a fire in the middle, a place at one end for the people, at the other end for the cows. In Ballymenone, the little piece of Ireland I know, the old house, like Mrs. Cutler's, set the dwelling, the stable for the horses, and the byre for the cows, in one long range. But there was no internal communication from one part to the other. Solid

In this longhouse, an instance of compressed design, the people live to the left, the cattle to the right of the chimney, under one roof. Dartmoor, Devonshire, England. 1972

Dispersal begins when the house separates from the working buildings. St. Hilary, Glamorgan, Wales. 1972

walls separated the house from the agricultural buildings attached to its ends. Modernizing farmers have torn the agricultural buildings down and rebuilt them. They preserve the old axial arrangement but increase the separation between the domestic and the agricultural by opening space between the buildings. The change in time, in Ireland as well as in Scotland, England, and Wales, leads away from compression and toward dispersal. The climate did not change.

For an example of a truly dispersed plan, the farm of the southern Midwest in the United States will do. Fences separate and enclose the farm as a whole. From the main road, a long lane leads to the buildings. A fence follows the lane and divides the farmstead into two separate spheres. One is centered upon the house, the other on the barn. The framed house is painted glossy white and ornamented modestly on the porch. Internally it offers a parlor to the front, a kitchen on the rear. Behind the house, small buildings stand in attendance upon the kitchen. The plain framed barn is weathered to gray or painted red, and around it cluster small agricultural buildings, a crib for corn, houses for poultry and hogs.

Formally in the longhouse, experientially in the open squares of Bangladesh and Sweden, domestic work mingles with agricultural work. On the Midwestern farm, kinds of work separate clearly in space and gather gendered associations. With a fence between its house and barn, the Midwestern farm displays a pattern that was developed in the countryside of Britain and North America, and then perfected during industrialization.

On the farm, domestic space, associated with a clean and comfortable life, becomes the woman's realm. The man leaves the house to the woman and goes to another place to do the work that is really work, the work that brings cash. The hunt for money brings him into the tanglement of capitalism. In Bengal, it is dramatically different. The plan unites the kitchen, the bedrooms, the shed for the cow, and the workshop. Within the open space these buildings define, one woman cooks dinner, the others join the men, fanning rice and making pots.

In planning, as in technology, the rural tradition of the West was exaggerated during industrialization. Clarifying the separation implicit in the farmstead by locating the place for work far from the place for living, industrialization bequeathed to us the stereotyped roles against which we fight with so little success.

If we shift up another level in design, from the familial to the communal, we will find the designers in Bengal and Dalarna again performing similarly. The square farmsteads pack tightly into a village, where buildings jumbled in numbers give the place a dense urban feel. Nearly continuous walls run along the lanes. Behind them, courtyards open for work, and then the lanes run out of the village, leading to a spacious countryside. There are no buildings. The fields spread wide. The family's land is parceled and scattered through the open fields. Divided but unfenced, the fields offer no hindrance to cooperation. Bits of tillage owned by neighbors interlock into a green mosaic of communal unity.

The communities of Bengal and Dalarna are both examples of the agricultural openfield village. It is the structural opposite of the dispersed landscapes of Ireland or the American Midwest. The openfield village consolidates housing and scatters the family's holdings. On the dispersed landscape, the houses are scattered and the family's holdings are consolidated in the fields that surround the dwelling.

Beyond the buildings of the village, beyond the open fields that fan around it, lie other places where members of the community exploit their customary rights. Bengalis use the river and its banks for bathing, beaching boats, and processing clay to make pottery. Swedish farmers cut timber on certain hillsides, and they have places in the high pastures where cattle are driven in the summer. Then the village builds connections beyond its communal space. Roads join the village to a market town, and more

Tibble. Leksand, Dalarna, Sweden. 1992

Kagajipara. Dhamrai, Bangladesh. 1995

roads join the town to the big city. Produce leaves along that route. Cash and goods and the world's new ideas return along it. The city needs the village — the source of its food — more than the village needs the city, but they interconnect in trade. They always have. The idea of isolation is an explanatory convenience in bad history. It dismisses village tradition as the product of ignorance, rather than recognizing it to be the product of choice, which it is.

Central to choice is the building not yet mentioned. Swedish villages connect into parishes. In the old days by communal boat, and now by private automobile, the people of different villages assemble in the parish church to hear the word of the Lord. In Bangladesh, villages are more likely to have their own mosques, but similarities continue. The villages on the delta of Bengal are separate entities, each built on a single foundation, a platform of clay raised by hand above the flood, each sheltered by a single roof, shaped by the trees that stand and branch to weave a canopy overhead. Then the villages straggle together on their mounds, as Swedish villages do along the main roads, and while many villages have mosques, other villages have no religious building, and the people of different villages assemble for worship in public mosques or Hindu temples.

Church, mosque, or temple, it is the largest, finest building of the community, constructed of materials more permanent than those of the houses, and decorated with donations made by members of the congregation. In this most firm and beautiful of environments, the word spoken is love. The sense of unity that people achieve in worship filters through all of life, giving them strength and restraint — the faith and trust of engaged existence. The sacred ideology of union, learned in the church or mosque or temple, becomes real in the cooperative arrangements that make village life possible, when people who do not necessarily like one another pray together on holy days, work together in the wide fields, and sit together at night, enduring again the dull company of those they choose to love.

Forms and Causes

Now, understanding something about building in Bangladesh and central Sweden, areas that are strikingly different in climate and prosperity, yet comparable in architecture, we can turn to causation. Founded upon faith, conjoining the familial with the communal, an idea of social order seems to be the prime condition of design when architects in Bengal or Dalarna plan relations among buildings. The environment sets an outer ring of constraint. Its conditions are brought into consideration whenever they do not contradict the more fundamental concerns that are sacred, social, and economic. There is logic in that formulation, but it is not so easy as that.

The most successful historical movement of our time, in my estimation, has been dedicated to the study of the landscape of the British Isles. By treating the land itself as the primary text and reading it closely during painstaking fieldwork, by building a geographical base for understanding and then bringing the more fragmentary and less democratic written record to bear during the construction of explanations, scholars have shaped a sweeping new view of history that attends to both continuity and change, while focusing on general cultural processes and not on the doings of a few errant princes. In England, W.G. Hoskins gave eloquent, public voice to the movement. In Ireland, the great spokesman was E. Estyn Evans.

One conclusion, reached early in the study of the English landscape, divided the whole into two zones. There was a highland pastoral zone of thin soil and steep slopes, where people lived in longhouses on separate farms, tending the cattle that grazed around them. There was a lowland agricultural zone of heavy, arable soil, where families drew together in tight villages and went out to work cooperatively in the open fields. The distinction is too neat, and generations of scholars have qualified it extensively in new research. But a great pattern remains. From

England, the island at one end of the Eurasian landmass, to Japan, the island at the other, when the soil is fit to the plow, people tend to settle in openfield villages.

Bengal and Dalarna are radically different in climate, but they share other environmental conditions. Both belong to the lowland zone. Both have good soil and open land. It rolls in Sweden, it is relentlessly flat in Bengal, but it is naturally disposed to agriculture. Processes differ in the dry cultivation of wheat and the wet cultivation of rice, but in the days before machinery — our days in Bangladesh — agricultural technology required energy to be built through human cooperation. And the need for cooperation led to compact settlement. And villages borrowed an economically useful ideology of oneness from religious scripture. But, of course, that is too simple. Were it an adequate explanation, the scholar's trim old division of the land into highland and lowland zones would not have gotten so muddled by later research.

If people responded, naturally or mechanically, to steep slopes and thin soil by settling on separate farms, then mountainous Anatolia would be, like the moorland of Devon, a place of longhouses deposited on independent steadings. The environment does not determine. It establishes one of the conditions of choice, and the Turks chose the communal way, settling the mountains in villages. The minaret points out of the mass of houses on the crest of a rocky ridge, or the houses run in terraced rows along the slope, facing downhill into the warmth. The fields spread into a green patchwork below. The gray mountain rises above, where sheep and goats pick among the rocks. The view is still more dramatic in northern Pakistan. There the valleys are sectioned into fields, and the mosque and the houses of the village cling to the steep sides of towering, snowy peaks. Although Ireland is a hilly display of separate farms, the pattern of rundale led in the rocky west to a clustering of houses and a division of fields comparable to Turkey's.

Paşaköy. Çanakkale, Turkey. 1990

Damlacık. Adıyaman, Turkey. 1989

In human affairs, it could always be different. People choose. Though their economy was pastoral, their land was steep and stony, the Turks chose the openfield village. They built villages, too, on the flat, fat lowlands, uniting their landscape into an objective demonstration of their option for community. That it was a choice, and not some force in the environment, is proved by places along the Black Sea where Turkish farmers live in dispersed settlements.

Turks choose to build villages in unsuitable places. Bengalis and Swedes choose to build villages on land right for agriculture. The land did not invent the plan. People brought the plan with them when they came, and they made it work in the places they settled.

If people always built compactly on land suitable for agriculture, then the United States would be largely a place of openfield villages. But in the mountains and on the plains, the United States is Turkey's opposite. It is unified by dispersed settlement. As in Turkey, there are exceptions that test the rule, reveal it to be imperfect, and prove that the landscape is shaped by willful action.

The American pattern of dispersal is interrupted by images of compression, compression so extreme that buildings come together, connect, and pile upon one another in the Native American villages of the Southwest. At Acoma, at Taos, at Cochiti and Santa Clara, the church stands aside when men and women carrying rattles and wisps of evergreen rise out of the kiva to dance in lines, separating and converging, transcribing the lineaments of a monumental sacred architecture in the dust and air. Their Hispanic neighbors built openfield villages on the European model. The Catholic church stands in the plaza, an open square enclosed by the houses that string along its sides. The fields, divided by allotment, run beyond into an open expanse.

The most spectacular exception to the American rule — oppositional by intention — is the Mormon village. Fine small farmhouses, Midwestern in form, stand on a foursquare grid like that of a Midwestern town, but the farmer's holdings are cast through

Pueblo. Taos, New Mexico. 1987

Plaza. San José, New Mexico. 1990

the fields that spread beyond the village. The vast, mountainous backdrop does little to disturb the comparison. Viewed across the fields, the village of Utah or southern Idaho, with its tall temple and low gathering of houses, offers an image out of old England. In medieval England and nineteenth-century Utah, villages were asserted into space by people who made clear-headed decisions. They chose to build as they did in order to exploit the environment efficiently through agriculture, and in order to shape a social order that brought the familial and the communal together on the base of the sacred.

By genetic dispensation, people are beings of memory, imagination, and will. They choose, and they live only in the world where every choice is made on a field of cause and consequence too large and complex to control or know completely. The result of choice is history.

History

In Virginia and in Massachusetts, the first English settlement was a village. Providing protection and a familiar experience, the village brought unity to the disparate populations gathered at Jamestown and Plymouth. At the time of settlement, early in the seventeenth century, the England they left was in the midst of the most revolutionary change since the Neolithic. Openfield villages a thousand years old still stood on the lowlands, but the process of enclosure, powered by money and law, was reordering the landscape.

The open fields were surveyed, divided, consolidated, and fenced — enclosed — and separate farms were created on the arable lowlands. Village people resisted, leveling new walls, uprooting new hedges, and formulating loose customs into firm traditions designed to counter the expansion of law. Their heroic actions attracted the attention and won the sympathy of intellectuals, and the study of custom and tradition, of folklore, was born in England.

Mormon Village. Paris, Idaho. 1990

Farm. Gardnersville, Nevada. 1989

Village. Braunton, Devon, England. 1978

Village houses. Boscastle, Cornwall, England. 1978

Village fields. Boscastle, Cornwall, England. 1978

Village houses. Kınık, Bilecik, Turkey. 1996

Village houses. Acoma, New Mexico. 1990

Farmstead. Emmen, Holland. 1972

Farmstead. County Down, Northern Ireland. 1972

Church in the Greek Revival style. Orange County, New York. 1968

Church in the Southwestern style. Picuris, New Mexico. 1971

Hall-and-parlor house. Madison County, Virginia. 1977

I-house. Etchison, Maryland. 1969

Village. Checkenden, Oxfordshire, England. 1972

Separate farm. King William County, Virginia. 1978

During enclosure, the power of the village people was great enough to slow things down, to force compromises, and to preserve some openfield villages from destruction. But theirs was the weaker power in the conflict. Their choices were canceled by choices made by people who had more money and better weaponry. The big pattern in time was clear.

On the landscape, the openfield village was replaced by the separate farm. The change from the village to the farm was a change in social order from the communal to the familial. In the village, the dwelling was part of a larger architectural composition that embedded the family securely in the community. On the landscape of separate farms, the dwelling stands alone, and people might or might not work to construct a larger community. The new pattern isolates the family.

The change from the village to the farm was a change from sacred to secular orders. The church standing at the center of the village was the source of the precepts that people used in constructing a customary order for life. On the landscape of separate farms, no church stands in view. People live apart, and local customs come into conflict and compromise with the civil codes devised by the state to increase its dominion. The new pattern replaces collaborative experience with secular doctrine, uniting isolated families by law and political order.

The change from the village to the farm was a change in the economy from collective to individual enterprise. In the village, maintenance was the goal, cooperation was the means, and cooperation required restraint and engendered trust. On the landscape of separate farms, the family works for itself, and its own energies and resources apparently set the only limits for its economic success. In the new pattern, the isolated family operates within a legal framework, and the goal is profit.

My summary is painfully schematic. Its purpose is not to erect categories, classifying the village as sacred, the farm as secular. The purpose is to reveal shifts in emphasis, tendencies in time that give us some purchase on the slow, tremendous change

Saint Brannock's. Braunton. 1978

during which one architectural form was replaced by another. Since architecture is not a system unto itself, the architectural change provides the clearest evidence of a cultural change that happened at different times in different places. That cultural change led from a communal order that mixed social and economic goals on a sacred base to an order in which profit took precedence, and the family was isolated as a unit of enterprise within a massive system based on the laws of the state and the needs of the capitalist.

That change is not inevitable. If it were, no villages would remain, and yet villages still dominate the agricultural landscape of Eurasia. In England, though, the openfield village is nearly gone. W. G. Hoskins estimated that half of England's arable land had been enclosed by 1700. When a single landlord owned the earth of the village, he let the farmers complete the harvest, then sent them packing in the winter's cold, demolishing their houses and collecting their strips of tillage into immense hedged pastures where sheep could graze, growing wool for sale. In villages where ownership was divided among many freeholders, they gathered, consolidated their fields, fenced them, and eventually built separate farmsteads. The process that private owners began was completed by the government in the eighteenth and nineteenth centuries. The four and a half million acres that had been open fields in 1700 were reduced to a few hundred when Hoskins wrote in 1955. He mentioned four villages that had survived somehow, and I followed his book to one of them, Braunton in Devon, where I lived for a few months in 1978.

The spire of Saint Brannock's ancient church lifts a golden cock over the tight rows of houses. At the corners, farmhouses stake out the neat plan of the town that was built by Anglo-Saxon pioneers next to the mission church founded by Saint Brannock. He sailed a stone across from Wales to bring the Good News to the heathens of Devon. At first he built on Chapel Hill, high above the valley cut by the River Caen. Every night his work was undone. Then God told him to build below, where he would find a sow with her farrow. At that fertile site, he built his church, and harnessing a team of wild deer to the task, Saint Brannock was the first to plow the rich alluvial soil. The church Saint Brannock built in the sixth century was rebuilt in the thirteenth. The open fields laid out in the eighth century, though diminished in scope and the number of holdings, remain to be seen. Braunton's Great Field is striped with long, curving strips, attached in random alternation to households in the village. Its sections are marked by bondstones, and its strips are separated only by narrow balks of grass called landsherds.

Braunton's view of history is put on display in an annual pageant. It takes place in the nave of the church, and it begins with the arrival of Saint Brannock, played by the priest, Father Budge. Then comes a long series of splendidly dressed kings and queens, who stand aside and do nothing, while the people of the village, played by the people of the village, do all the action and have all the fun. Their play, like their church building, exhibits the mutability of fashion and temporal power, and the stability of common life.

The farmers of Braunton know their place is unusual, but their question is not how their big prosperous village survived. It is why other people changed from the village to the agricultural units they call "ring-fence farms."

Ernie Hartnoll, whose family has worked Town Farm since the days of the Domesday survey, answered his own question when he told me that openfield villages, like his Braunton, are "bad for farming, but good for farmers." He meant that it is hard to manage an efficient operation when the farmer, moving on his tractor from one of his fields to another, gets stuck in traffic, but the village is good for human beings. Children can walk to school and play with their mates in the fresh air. Women are not shut up in a farmhouse, far from their neighbors; they visit casually, do their shopping on foot, and run the businesses of the village. At night, men and women walk to their local, greet the landlord, and lift a few pints with their friends.

Braunton, the view from Chapel Hill:
St. Brannock's below, the Great Field on the horizon.

Landsherd separating holdings on Pitlands field.
The Great Field. Braunton, Devon, England. 1978

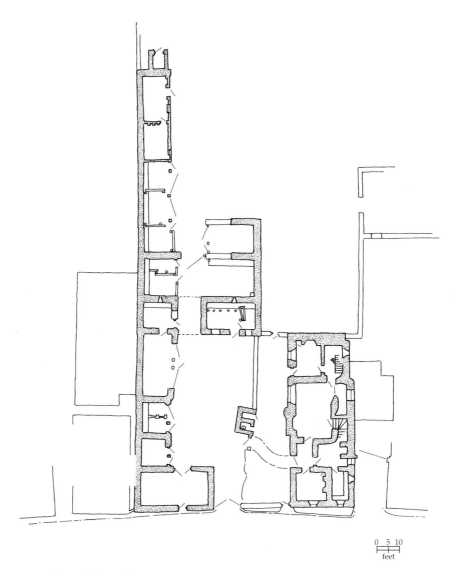

0 5 10
feet

Town Farm. Braunton.
Ernie Hartnoll's Town Farm exemplifies the village pattern that England
shares with Sweden and Bangladesh. The farmstead (above) collects the
main buildings around a courtyard, the house to the right, the barn, shop,
and stable to the left. The shippen for cows closes the courtyard, then
sheds for pigs on the right, carts, root crops, and chickens on the left, run
toward the orchard in the rear. It is located on North Street in the town.
The fields (see the map on the facing page) are scattered south and east.

Braunton. Devonshire, England.
The railroad and the new highway that cut along the River Caen have been omitted to reveal the old plan. A dotted line shows the extent of the village in 1978. St. Brannock's Church is marked by a cross. Buildings strung along the old streets are hatched. Town Farm is black. Town Farm's dispersed holdings are stippled, arable in the Great Field to the southwest, pastures on Braunton Down to the east.

Bad economically, an impediment to enterprise, the village is good socially. It yielded to arrangements that were the reverse when profit took command.

England's change has not happened, and will not happen, everywhere. But the pattern in time is by no means restricted to England. In southern Sweden, the village was replaced by the farm, exactly as in England. What makes Dalarna in central Sweden so distinct, so special in the Swedish view of nationhood, is that the farmers of Dalarna fought the agents of change, and openfield villages, like those in the very different environments of Turkey and Bangladesh, remain common.

The American Landscape

The purpose of this excursion has been to understand the choice that made the American landscape. Living in villages in Jamestown and Plymouth, English people understood village life, and they knew of an alternative: enclosure. In both places, they abandoned the village for separate farms. They did not risk their lives on a black ocean to repeat the old but to create the new. They came to get rich. Religious rhetoric and the resistance of the native people could retard but not stop the spread of enclosure.

Jamestown and Plymouth might have been twin points of origin for a landscape unified by enclosure. Instead, history led to regional difference. In New England, the Puritans fought dispersal and isolation, returning by choice to the openfield village. They located a meetinghouse at the center of town and scattered tillage in strips through the open fields, rededicating themselves to the way of the Lord. New England developed in tension between the opposed energies of compression and dispersal. Villages predominated in some areas, notably the lowlands of the Connecticut Valley. In other places, high, rough, and marginal, the farmhouses stood alone. The scene in the South was simpler. Houses, churches, and even courthouses stood apart. Old Virginia was the first impeccably capitalistic landscape.

Pennsylvania, last to be settled and culturally most diverse, presents a swelling, green landscape of separate farms. In Pennsylvania, a synthesis of German, English, and Irish practice was established on independent family farms, and that pattern — call it American — was perfected in the Valley of Virginia and then extended through the Midwest. As time passed and people pressed westward, regional differences diminished. In the wake of genocide, the land of the interior was surveyed, gridded, and enclosed. States have cities, counties have towns, the countryside spreads with separate family farms.

Then as the skies widened and dried, the farms expanded in size. The ranch of the West was like the plantation of the South, a commercial operation in the open air, an immense factory without walls. The owner hires a boss, the boss directs the hands, and they produce a commodity — cattle, protein on hoof, rather than the tobacco or cotton or sugar of the plantation, or the clocks and locks and firearms of the compact, mechanized factories of old New England. The widening dispersal was not ordered by a sacred, communal vision, but by civil law and a network of trade.

A white wooden steeple points above a gathering of white wooden farmhouses: the village was a reality in New England, and it lingers dimly in the historical imagination, tempering free enterprise slightly with vague talk about community values, and occasionally inspiring evanescent experiments in communal living. The Mormons revived the idea of the village in the West. A few urban neighborhoods have the old village feel. But the big pattern was clear from the beginning, and it endures in subdivisions, called estates or ranches or parks, where houses stand in isolation, each on its own grassy plot.

The American landscape says that people chose to exchange the confidence of communal life for the excitement of the pursuit for wealth. In daily experience, it might have been only a gentle, nearly imperceptible shift in common conduct as people worked and lived in contentment among their neighbors. In history, it was a great watershed.

113

The people had chosen. At the communal level of design, they shifted from compressed to dispersed arrangements. When we move down a level, we will find the same culture at work, trading compressed plans, in which many functions combine, for dispersed plans in which functions separate by logical category. Before the philosophers, the rural builders were hell-bent rationalists.

Advancing the cause of enclosure on lowland terrain, American farmers chose change. When people came from the uplands of Europe, looking for land they knew how to use, and then settled the American uplands with separate farms, their actions can be taken as continuous. But change was trapped in continuity. Keeping to tradition, they should have built longhouses in the mountainy wilderness as people did in the pioneering phase of British settlement. Instead, they planned their farms into division, setting the house here, the barn there, and surrounding each of them with ancillary outbuildings.

At the communal level, they chose dispersal over compression, isolating the family. Similarly favoring dispersal in planning the farm, they divided the family unit into its domestic and working halves. In the United States, highland and lowland zones are alike in their separate farms, and they are alike in farms that separate the house from the barn.

Tax records from the end of the eighteenth century provide two instances of buildings in Pennsylvania that housed the people and their cattle under one roof. Two out of many thousands: a dramatic change had been completed in two generations. In the areas of Central Europe from which the Pennsylvania Germans came, buildings analogous to the longhouses of Britain, buildings that were dwellings and barns at once, were the norm. Although German immigrants constructed a few unified buildings in eighteenth-century Pennsylvania, as they would in nineteenth-century Wisconsin and Missouri, they developed for themselves a distinct version of the general American practice. They continued to build the house and barn in a line, but rather

Cumberland County, Pennsylvania. 1971

Frederick County, Maryland. 1972

than attaching them, they separated them, like the modernizing farmers of Ballymenone. From southeastern Pennsylvania, through central Maryland, and into the Valley of Virginia, the house and barn align along a slope, facing downhill toward the sun. The farther west and south they went, the more likely the house was to be English in origin, but the big beautiful barn was Germanic, and the two of them stood together, separated by fences and open space. Their alignment recalls the unified buildings of Europe. Their separation makes them fit America, where the domestic separated from the agricultural, making way for industrialization.

There must be exceptions, and Thomas Hubka has documented one of them handsomely. In northern New England, during the nineteenth century, farmers moved their houses and barns into connection in a hopeless effort to restore order during defeat. Prosperity had gone west to flat farmland where the big machines could roll, where agriculture and industrial capitalism could come into productive collusion.

The wish for separation, displayed on the landscape of separate farms and on farms that separate the house from the barn, will continue to drive planning when we shift down a level, to the domestic.

An Entry to History

I discovered history in houses. In 1966, I selected a small area in the middle of Virginia for study. A wide, loose survey convinced me that the area would make a good sample of the large architectural region of the Chesapeake Bay. Acting happily within the frame for research crafted by my mentor Fred Kniffen, I intended to depict the geographical personality of the region through its buildings. I made a quick record of every house and drew careful measured plans of many. Old houses dutifully exhibited a distinct regional character, but the more I analyzed them, the more I felt that the big story was historical change. My training in social science, in days dominated by synchronic systematizing, did little to prepare me for the job at hand.

Houses spoke of history. The old house had a square hall with a narrower parlor built on its end. The front door gave access immediately to the interior, and it was set a touch off center to expose the internal workings to view. With one step, the visitor enters the hall, then turns toward the fire where the work of cooking and entertainment takes place.

The new house was a type that Fred Kniffen named the I-house, achieving immortality by contributing a word to the common language. Two stories high, but only one room deep, the I-house is tall and slender in profile, like the letter. The I-house presents a wide bilaterally symmetrical facade that hides the interior. One side looks like the other, and it is hard to say where you will go once you get in. Upon entering, you do not stand in a room where people sit. You are in an unheated, unlit corridor — a hallway, a way to the hall — out of which you must be led to the sociable place.

Choosing to build a new house instead of an old one is a progressive step, a stretch perhaps for status. But anything can be made to signify status. The tiny teahouse that was designed to evoke poverty and the hermit's hut were buildings of high status in aristocratic Japan. Analysis should not be displaced by quick ascriptions of status. What we need to know, through formal analysis, is what changes during change. The shift from the hall-and-parlor house to the I-house was a compositional move in massing from the organic to the geometric. The change in massing disrupts entry, separating insiders from outsiders. Separation was accomplished internally by the hallway and externally by the facade. The hall-and-parlor house offers a gently asymmetrical array of openings that reveal the interior. The front of the I-house covers the interior with a geometric image of order.

I found old houses smaller than the hall-and-parlor house, some with only one room. Small houses are less likely to survive than large ones, so we can imagine many more in the past, but enough remained to exemplify their forms. I found houses larger than the I-house, some with the heavy double-pile depth of the Georgian ideal, rather than the slim plan of the I-house that balances one room on each side of the hallway. The house of one room and the Georgian mansion stood at the opposite ends of a scale of size, which probably approximated a scale of wealth, but these antiquarian details do nothing to alter the pattern of change that led from open to closed plans, and from asymmetrical to symmetrical facades.

Features once restricted to the rare mansions of the gentry began to become general in domestic design during the 1760s, a time of intensifying tension. Determining that the architectural change in the Chesapeake region took place on the eve of the American Revolution, I interpreted the shift from one house to the other as material evidence of the change in social arrangements that brought the war that built the nation. Houses told of a retreat from the community of immediate experience, where people might be radicals, loyalists, or unconcerned, where differences were stiffening along lines of class and race and persuasion — it was a time of hot revival and cool deism, of conflict between the old Church and the New Light.

If order is lacking in the world, if the people mingling in space cannot be trusted to carry order within themselves, if their conduct is threatening or impolite, then order must be built into buildings that block and direct them. The I-house stopped people and channeled them with its hallway. Then compensating for experiential disorder with conceptual order, it projected an abstract and rational message on its facade. At once tripartite and bilaterally symmetrical, divisible by both odd and even numbers, the front of the I-house puts on public display a unified image that firmly contains division. The facade was designed on principles that traditionally — on the cathedral, in the carving and painting of furniture, in the structure of the folktale and ballad, in the ranking of society — signal the presence of control in communication.

Change in Virginia.

Above: Open and asymmetrical; left, partitioned house of one bay; right, hall-and-parlor house. Below: Closed and symmetrical; left, I-house; right, Georgian house. This is an early example; the conventional Georgian house has back rooms equal in size to the front rooms and a hallway consistent in width. The I-house most often has a facade with three openings per floor, like the hall-and-parlor house, though it was also built with five openings in the Georgian manner. Characteristically, the hall-and-parlor house has one story, though it was also built in two-story versions. The I-house and Georgian house are characteristically two stories high, though, especially south of Virginia, one-story houses have plans like I-houses and Georgian houses.

Hall-and-parlor house. Louisa County, Virginia. 1973

I-house. Surry County, Virginia. 1975

The architectural change fit the times. Trading the immediate community for an abstract vision out of which a new union could be built, the I-house in Virginia was one symptom of the change in the hearts and minds of men that made the Revolution. The old house belonged to the little community of engagement, of constant and direct exchange. The new house belonged to an overarching concept of manifest and self-evident reason — to a political nation as yet unborn. The farmers acted. The politicians got the message and followed along, completing the process later in a tripartite, symmetrically composed constitution.

My idea, however uncongenial to conventional presumptions about leaders and followers in history, gained support through architectural comparison. When I was trying to make sense of the data in Virginia, I had not yet been to England, and new to history, I still thought of temporal developments in national terms. The most obvious and provocatively supportive comparison did not cross my mind. In southern England, there was a pronounced shift from organic to geometric massing before the English Revolution. My thinking at the time turned to places in America I did know. Building houses that were internally closed by a hallway and masked externally by a symmetrical facade, people in Virginia came into alignment with people in New England.

Old England differs regionally in its traditional housing. As is the case in Ireland, houses with chimneys in the middle dominate toward the east, houses with chimneys on the gable ends dominate in the west. The patterning, through, is not sharp in England. English immigrants to America would have known of both ways to build, and there was much architectural diversity during the first phase of settlement. But slowly American regions consolidated and peeled apart.

In New England and Virginia, the common plan united a hall with a parlor. But the chimney was set in the middle in New England, between the hall and parlor, and chimneys flanked the ends of the house in Virginia, one for the hall, one for the parlor.

Both regions exhibit continuity. People from the east of England came to New England, people from the west of England came to Virginia, and they settled into their new places with familiar dwellings. It takes great exertion to preserve continuity despite differences of space and time, but the volition of the early builders becomes easier to appreciate when we note that their choices were environmentally correct. They knew different kinds of houses, and they eventually selected the right one for the weather. In cold New England, the central chimney radiates heat throughout the house. In hot Virginia, chimneys set at the ends of the house leave its center open to the circulation of air through opposed doors and windows.

If environmental adaptation during continuity told the whole story, then the architects of New England would have built the kind of house that was most common in southeastern England. It would have worked in the climate, for its chimney was located between the hall and the parlor. Then, on the usual house of southeastern England, a third room opened off the hall, standing in service to the hearth during the preparation of food. Service, hall, parlor: these three spaces were arranged in a neat line in the narrow houses of England. But architects in New England did not build houses like that. Instead, they chose a rare form from southeastern England and brought it to dominance in New England. Their house, the saltbox house, seems quaint today, but in the early seventeenth century, it was the newest of all English houses, streamlined and ultramodern.

In the saltbox house, the service wing was moved from the end to the rear and covered by the long descent of the roof that gives the house its profile and name. The first effect of this change is a separation between insiders and outsiders. With the service wing out of sight on the rear, the facade can be composed in perfect tripartite, bilateral symmetry. It baffles entry. Open the door, and you are baffled again. You are not in a room. You are in a vestibule, like the lobby of the Swedish house that keeps chilly

The typical house
of southeastern
England.
Robertsbridge,
East Sussex.
1982

Saltbox house.
Southminster,
Essex, England.
1973

Saltbox. Southampton, Long Island. 1970

winds out, and you are in a social lock, like the hallway of later Virginia, that keeps unwelcome visitors out.

The second effect of the saltbox plan is a separation made among the people who live inside. Attached to the rear of the house, the service wing gains access to the central chimney. It becomes a full working kitchen. Formerly the hall mixed cooking and entertainment. The lofty hall of the Wealden house, like the kitchen of the houses in Ballymenone, was at once the kitchen and the living room. The new arrangement relieves the hall of work, leaving it cleaner, and it purifies the kitchen into a place for domestic labor. If the family has servants, then differences between the householders and the servants clarify in architectural fabric. If the family has no servants, then someone from the family must be designated a servant, removed from the social arena of the hall, and exiled to a smoky back place. Class and gender distinctions merge and harden.

When the functions that were compressed in the hall are dispersed through the house, a particular point has been reached in history. Division will elaborate in the future when a dining room is added, but the arrival of a second kitchen, a place for cooking meals that is distinct from the place for entertainment, allows us to date with precision the moment when the gender roles of modern times came into being. Together with the separation of the barn from the house, the advent of the second kitchen tells us that the roles, which some consider natural and eternal, were constructed in our culture not so long ago.

Selected out of the English repertory for use in seventeenth-century New England, the saltbox house was a thoroughly modern creation. It presented a symmetrical facade, a closed interior, and a second kitchen.

When a new form arrived in the eighteenth century, New England builders doubled their options. Called Georgian, for it became common in the long period when men named George sat on England's throne, the new form was an English version of

124

The Georgian house of New England. Sag Harbor, Long Island. 1970

The New England compromise: saltbox interior in a Georgian box, with Greek Revival trim. Portsmouth, New Hampshire. 1976

a Dutch version of an Italian version of an original from the eastern Mediterranean. The Georgian form offered a symmetrical facade and a central hallway. It was familiar enough to gain easy acceptance, yet new enough to serve as a symbol of fashion and progress. From the environmental standpoint, it was foolish to trade the central chimney, a source of heat, for a central hallway designed to move the air in hot climates. But the Georgian form worked socially like the saltbox house, separating insiders from outsiders and putting the kitchen to the rear. And like the saltbox house in its day, the Georgian house was all the rage. So some people built Georgian houses. For them, clearly, fashion and social order mattered more than the climate. But more people compromised cleverly, stuffing their old interior into a new box, symmetrical from the side as well as the front, and betrayed as old-fashioned, and environmentally sane, by the big chimney that poked above the roof in the middle.

During the Georgian period, the new houses of New England and Virginia were closed internally by a lobby or a hallway, and they were masked by a symmetrical facade. Continuities with past practice left the regions distinct. In Virginia, the chimneys of the I-house, like those of the hall-and-parlor house, were built externally on the ends, in the western English manner. In New England, the chimney rose through the middle of the house, as it did in eastern England, or a fashionable hallway bisected the house, and when it did, the chimneys were not usually set on the ends, as they were in Virginia. They conserved heat by standing internally between the front and rear rooms. But the differences were slight, the similarities great.

Once the houses of the North and South had gained symmetrical facades, they were subjected to a process of compositional segmentation that brought New England and Virginia together with Pennsylvania. The plan was fractured along its internal partitions to create houses that were conceptually parts of houses. By eliminating the rooms to one side of the central chimney or the central hallway, designers created a narrow house,

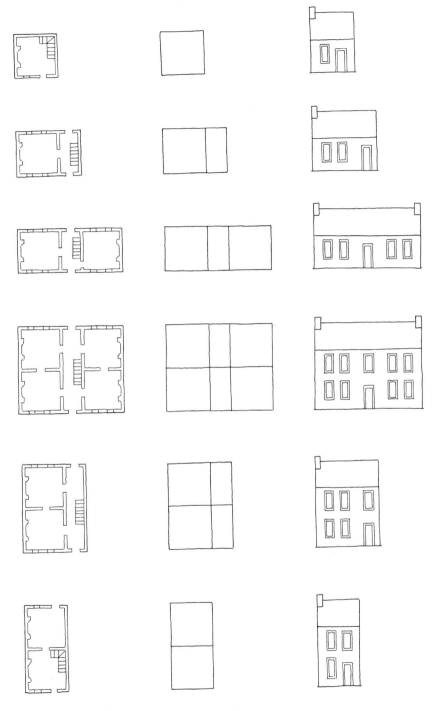

The system of segmentable symmetry.
Houses combine plans from the left column with facades from the right.

Two-thirds of the New England central-chimney house. East Hampton, Long Island. 1970

Two-thirds of an I-house. Winchester, Virginia. 1975

One-third of an I-house. Crisfield, Maryland. 1969

two-thirds of the whole, that suited cramped city lots. They did not stop there. The old urban house of England arranged the hall and parlor in single file, one behind the other. Designers rationalized that old house into one-third of the Georgian form, producing the terraced houses that typify English cities on both sides of the Atlantic; Philadelphia's streets are lined with them. The process by which houses were designed for city living unified urban and rural America within a single system of architectural options.

The fractional house solved the problem of tight urban space. It also solved the problem of limited resources in the countryside, providing less prosperous people with a way to participate in the big architectural change. In Virginia, even the smallest dwellings — the cabins built by slaves on the plantations and the cabins built out of logs by farmers on the slopes of the Blue Ridge — were brought into alignment. Of one room and one story, they were redesigned to be one-twelfth of the Georgian mansion. Architecture told you exactly where you stood in the unified order. With one square room, one chimney, one window, and one door, you were at the bottom. And architecture trained your aspirations. Your small house was not a miniaturized version of a large one, doomed for all time to smallness, as houses often were in England. It was a full-scale fragment of a big house. In time, it would expand with a shed on the rear, perhaps another room on the end. People of modest means built houses in the countryside that were one-third or two-thirds of the whole, and sometimes their heirs got lucky and added to the house, completing the scheme. The prevailing symmetry of the system marked asymmetry as incomplete, and it pushed action toward the achievement of logical unity.

The segmentable, symmetrical box, developed first in New England, came to unify the landscape of the eastern seaboard. The pattern appears wherever symmetry rules, but I have found it to be common in only one other place. On the island of Guernsey, houses also changed from open to closed plans, and from asymmetrical to symmetrical facades. The symmetrical house of Guernsey — an I-house exactly — was also segmented, not only in the usual way, by having one story instead of two, but in the American way too: the house might be a full one, with a room on either side of a central hallway, or it might be two-thirds of the whole, with a hallway to the side that provides a roundabout entry to the room next to it.

Guernsey supports the thrust of my argument. Like America, Guernsey is divided from England by water, and like America, it is culturally heterogeneous. The segmentable, symmetrical house overarched tense differences between English and French people on Guernsey, as it overarched differences between English and German people where they met in Pennsylvania, and as it overarched differences of wealth and persuasion in New England and Virginia. Replacing experiential confusion with abstract reason, a single architectural system brought houses into unity. It ranked them within a single order. It contained and directed progressive motion.

Closed, symmetrical, segmentable houses unified the American land, but regional differences were not at an end. Pennsylvania had its German sections, with houses that refused to fit neatly into the Georgian order. The North was a place of big houses, the South of big spaces. The landscape of Virginia had become modern, wholly enclosed, when designers in New England were still planning medieval villages. The architects of New England had settled on a fully modern dwelling, the saltbox house, when Southerners were still building houses that admitted visitors directly in the medieval way. A piece of the explanation is that Northern houses, set close together, used partitions to do what Southern houses, set far apart, used spatial expanse to do — to divide people from one another. In housing, though, New England got there first. But Virginians and Pennsylvanians were catching up, and the regions came into alignment, just when alignment was necessary, on the eve of the American Revolution.

Through architectural comparison, Virginia has become part of a massive, transatlantic region, unified by historical action. By breaking the village into separate farms, by breaking the longhouse into a house and a barn, by breaking the house out of contact with a facade and hallway, and then fragmenting its interior by function, people had broken up their little world, and they were ready to break up the big one. First they killed the king in England. Then they rebelled in America.

Comparison in Ireland

Thinking like that about the architectural change in Virginia, I proposed to test the idea with something like science. I knew from the superb writings of E. Estyn Evans that Ireland divided into two great architectural regions. The houses of the east, where the English settled, had central chimneys and linear plans like those of southeastern England. The houses of the Celtic west had chimneys on the ends, and they were socially open and pierced asymmetrically like the hall-and-parlor houses of Virginia. I knew, as well, that the Georgian form was introduced to Ireland in the eighteenth century, just as it was in Virginia. My idea was this: though it was present on the landscape, the Georgian form would not become adopted into common building practice until the people were ready, until they were ready to trade the little community they knew for an abstract concept that would bring them into national alliance with people they did not know. That, I surmised, would happen a decade or so before the successful revolution of 1916.

My hypothesis was this: along the border in western Ireland, houses would change from open to closed and from asymmetrical to symmetrical at the beginning of the twentieth century. The cause would be a hardening of political commitment that turned the neighbors away from each other, built factions, broke the community, and shaped new domestic arrangements in advance of the shaping of a national political order. Since writers at the time did not describe the newer houses, I could learn whether I was right only by going to Ireland.

In 1972, I settled in Ballymenone in southwestern Ulster, where my research would go on for a decade. The forms I found were not the forms I predicted. The old house was socially open and asymmetrical, right enough, but it was unlike the western Irish house of the books, and I took it for English in origin. As for the new house: I was expecting a country Georgian form that resembled the I-house. There are I-houses in eastern Ireland, but the new house in Ballymenone did not strike a hallway through the center. The hallway ran transversely, like the hallways in the houses of the Scottish Highlands. It looked different but worked comparably. Like the lobby of New England or the hallway of Virginia, it disrupted entry by setting an intermediate space between the world outside and the kitchen inside. And when the hallway came, the facade took on a tripartite, bilaterally symmetrical configuration. And soon after, the house sprouted a second kitchen on the rear.

In functional terms, the change in Ireland was precisely like the change in Virginia, and it happened exactly when I thought it would. The big difference was that I could know much more about the Irish change. I did not have to construct motives out of analysis. I could talk to people. They taught me generously, and my thinking was much improved.

Dating stumped me in Virginia. I dated undated buildings on analogy with dated ones in the wider region. In Ireland, people could tell me when houses were built. The first house of the new kind was built in 1900, and it was built by a Protestant policeman in a largely Catholic neighborhood — exactly the kind of person who would wish to withdraw behind a symmetrical facade. The last house of the old kind was built in 1958. The change took a long time in Ireland, and I see now that it took longer in Virginia than I had guessed.

Without intimate knowledge of community doings in eighteenth-century Virginia, I had to make a stretch to connect a

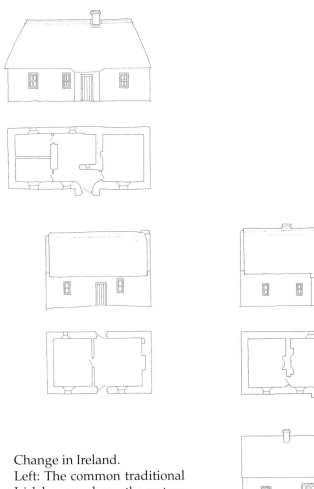

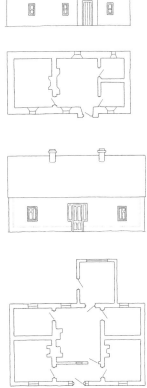

Change in Ireland.
Left: The common traditional Irish houses; above, the eastern type; below, the western type. Both of those types appear, though rarely, in Ballymenone. Right: The common houses of Ballymenone; above, the old type, open and asymmetrical; below, the new type, closed and symmetrical with a second kitchen on the rear.

Ballymenone's old house (see also p. 57).
Bellanaleck, Fermanagh, Northern Ireland. 1972

Ballymenone's new house (see also p. 43).
Springfield, Fermanagh, Northern Ireland. 1972

local change with the big changes recorded by historians. In Ballymenone, people could tell me about the small events that transferred big historical patterns into community life. When the first house of the new kind was built in Ballymenone, the large argument was about the relationship of Mother England to her colony, just as it was in Virginia when the I-house was invented out of the Georgian pattern. The little event that brought the big argument into Ballymenone was Billy Price attacking the band.

Here is the story as Hugh Nolan and Michael Boyle told it to me. A wealthy Protestant land owner suddenly decided not to rent two fields to the Catholic priest as he had in the past. Catholic farmers gathered and marched to a Protestant pub, beating drums and playing flutes, mounting a musical boycott. On their way home, they passed a field where a Protestant farmer, one Billy Price, was at work with a graip, turning sods. He was so enraged that he took up the weapon and attacked the band. Billy Price got a drubbing, and the boys of the band threw rocks through his windows, wrecking his house. That was the environment in which a Protestant policeman decided to build a new kind of dwelling.

Differences between radicals and loyalists, between Protestants and Catholics sharpened, and the revolution in the future did not resolve the issue in Ulster, as your newspaper will tell you. Increasingly both Catholics and Protestants chose to build houses on the new model. It was that kind of house that Tommy Moore built for Paddy McBrien in 1944. New starts were not common, but remodeling was, and most people — not all, but most — chose to add an enclosed porch, built of concrete blocks, to the front of the house that did outside what the hallway did inside.

The new house separates people from their neighbors — and it offers a truce. Standing alone, the house presents on its front a sign of rational order that transcends communal differences. The porch outside or the hallway inside becomes a transitional place where people, perhaps opposed in political orientation, can negotiate their differences politely.

In Ballymenone, I understood the architectural change much better. The old house welcomes everyone, and some people, especially those living far from the public routes through the community, continued to live in houses of the old kind in my days. The door was open. People walked in. The host trusted them to behave properly. They sat down and took tea. The new house acknowledges disorder. Standing near the public routes, the house makes it difficult to get inside. But once the guests have found their way to the hearth, they sit, drink tea, and the chat circles in the same old way. The new house enables continuity. But its people say that things have changed, and changed for the worse. They miss the easy exchanges of the past, but they live in this world, not that one, and the new house helps them manage.

Intimate information permitted me to refine my ideas of cause and effect in Ballymenone. The cause is immediate social disorder. The result is an object that compensates for disorder with devices that increase privacy and offer public symbols of conceptual order. The object marks the historical instant of a shift in cultural priorities. It dates the arrival of modernity.

When the enclosed landscape carries an open house, as it did in western Ireland and early Virginia, or when the compact village incorporates a closed house, as in Dalarna or early New England, the message is mixed. But when the fields are enclosed and the house is closed, the modern world has been created. Community is not dead, but it has lost dominance, and families live within political and economic systems that are too complex and expansive to understand or command. Social order dissolves, and the individual takes control, responsibly building a house that asserts an honorable point of rationality in a context of chaos.

Since the architectural change was so recent in Ballymenone, I was able to see clearly how the change in housing was one in a chain of changes. In Virginia, I could only drop general patterns into the void that opened before the time of the hall-and-parlor house. I could see the great change of enclosure, and I could see the pattern of environmental adaptation within continuity as people came and built houses in Virginia that were formally like those in England.

But in Ballymenone I learned that the change from open to closed houses followed hard upon another change. During that earlier change, houses of the old type were rebuilt in permanent materials. Wonderful new archaeological research in Virginia reveals that, in the time before the period of the buildings I examined, houses had been constructed of posts stuck in the soil, as they still are in Bangladesh. Then they were framed upon masonry foundations, rebuilt in more permanent materials. In Ireland, the modest old house was built with mud walls, or it was framed of jointed crucks impaled in the earth. As in Virginia, the old technology continued to be used in outbuildings, but the houses in Ballymenone became solid and permanent. Whitewash covered walls of stone or brick, and once houses were permanent, the local designers turned slowly then to symmetrical fronts and fragmented interiors.

It was not at first a double change. Impermanent and permanent materials were both local, taken from the land and processed by hand. But the wish for permanence established a precondition for the acceptance of imported, expensive, industrial materials.

The conditions of the shift from impermanent to permanent materials are patently clear in Ireland. The change happened in the era of the Land League's victory, during the last quarter of the nineteenth century. A massive meeting of the Land League took place right in Ballymenone. The Chief, the great Parnell himself, stood on the hill behind the thatched home of Hugh Patrick Owens and addressed a vast crowd of local farmers. Then, Hugh Patrick told me, they marched and fought and won for themselves the right to own the land they worked. Owning the land, he said, secure in their tenure, the people then built houses permanently upon it. The despicable landlord no longer owned the house. The people who lived in the house owned it outright, and it was worth their effort to rebuild the walls in firm materials and to make the interior more comfortable.

Now think of farmers in Virginia. They have come to a wild new place. It is not theirs, nor a landlord's, but nature's. They build expediently and work the land. At last, gaining wealth enough from agricultural labor, feeling secure in their tenure, they rebuild the old house, making it solid and fine. Then as differences in wealth mingle with differences in political and religious orientation, and community life becomes untenable, they rebuild again.

The sequence of change — from impermanent to permanent, from open to closed — locates the houses of Ireland and Virginia in the big pattern with which Eric Mercer frames his excellent book on the vernacular houses of England. In the beginning, the house was impermanent. At the end, it is permanent. In the middle of that pattern lies the transitional moment that W. G. Hoskins called the Great Rebuilding. In England, at different times, in different places, the walls of the houses were rebuilt in permanent materials and their interiors were fragmented by partitions. An early product of that change was the saltbox house, developed out of the Wealden house late in the sixteenth century in southern England. Later products include the I-house of eighteenth-century Virginia and the new house of twentieth-century Ballymenone.

The United States in the Nineteenth Century

Returning to the American story, we can envision a moment of unity, the most coherent instant in American history, when after the Revolution segmentable houses with symmetrical facades and closed interiors could be found from one end of the new nation to the other. That is as modern as things ever got.

In his excellent introduction to American architecture, Dell Upton comments correctly that the nineteenth century has been studied less well than the centuries that precede and follow it.

Nineteenth-century house
in the Georgian form.
Veazie, Maine. 1978

Nineteenth-century house
in the Georgian form with
Gothic and Italianate trim.
Oley, Pennsylvania. 1979

Nineteenth-century I-house with a Gothic gable.
Albemarle County, Virginia. 1966

One reason is that scholars seem to believe that the directions apparent in the eighteenth century continue through the nineteenth. Another is that, with the nineteenth century, there is a sudden flood of paper with words printed on it, and historians can relax at home, reading written texts that are easy to understand instead of the architectural texts that give them fits. But there is absolutely no alternative to fieldwork, to direct and patient study of real buildings in great numbers. The written texts of the nineteenth century are pertinent, but, alas, the story conveniently constructed out of them violently misrepresents the reality.

In a simplified telling, the eighteenth century was a time of convergence. The nineteenth century was a time of divergence, of the simultaneity of many big patterns at once.

One pattern was continuity. Up in the high blue mountains of the South, people continued to build open houses through the nineteenth century. Their small farms connected along the ridges and creeks into loose communities like Ireland's. Set apart, their wooden houses, built on old Irish or English plans, welcomed neighbors directly to the hearth. They stood in knowing contrast to the I-houses on the big farms in the valleys, separating the mountaineers who fought for union from the tuckahoes of the lowlands who fought for slavery's cause.

Down in eastern Virginia, builders seem to have achieved what they wanted in the I-house. It must have suited their sense of propriety, and they continued to build it in the new century. The Civil War came, devastated the land, and ended. In the new era after the war, Virginians built I-houses. There is nothing magical about turns of the century: I-houses were built into the 1930s. Northern New England also displays continuity. Houses with eighteenth-century plans were built before the Civil War and after the Civil War. In many rural places, 1880 would make a better end to the eighteenth century than 1800.

A second pattern was an extension of the eighteenth-century process into new territory. In some of the areas where houses remained open and asymmetrical, they were brought into the new order during the nineteenth century. In the hilly Piedmont of Virginia and North Carolina, people replaced medieval houses with eighteenth-century houses about 1850. Chris Wilson has documented the same change as taking place in the urban housing of Hispanic New Mexico between 1870 and 1910.

A third pattern involved the dismantling of the eighteenth-century accomplishment. In the Southern Appalachian region, throughout the southern Midwest, and in the West, notably in Mormon Utah, people built houses of the I-house kind, but they diminished the bulk. The house stood less than a full two stories high. Its symmetrical facade promised a central hallway, but, by eliminating one of the side walls of the hallway, the builders opened the interior to old hall-and-parlor patterns of use. From the Tennessee Valley westward and southward, architects brought about a similar change in a different way. They built geometrically massed houses with central corridors, but they omitted the front and rear walls of the hallway to create the dog-trot house. Good in hot weather, the dogtrot house sucks the exterior into the interior. The wide open hallway — people who live in such houses call it a hall, not a dogtrot — makes a fine place for cool sitting and casual visiting.

When the eighteenth-century plan was dismantled, the result blended the old and the new. A similar compromise characterizes a fourth pattern — one of fresh design. Presented at the end of the eighteenth century with the Georgian concept, architects redesigned medieval houses so that they had apparently symmetrical facades, but rather than centering a door between windows, they brought two doors to the front so that the house could be entered directly in the old way. That is the pattern of the saddlebag house of the Southern Appalachian domain, of the Deep South, and the southern Midwest. And it is the pattern of houses built by German people in Pennsylvania and French people in Louisiana.

German house.
York County,
Pennsylvania.
1967

Saddlebag house.
Stokes County,
North Carolina.
1965

Shotgun houses. Louisville, Kentucky. 1994

The people who designed the fresh compromises in the nineteenth century are customarily neglected in simple national narratives. Southern Mountaineers, Pennsylvania Dutch, Cajuns in Louisiana — these are the people the old folklorists approached in their search for ancient songs and stories. Their houses provide tangible, measureable, objective evidence of the presence among them of something that brings them together and separates them from the historian's mainstream.

The people who are obviously missing from the list in the last paragraph created a fifth pattern, one of a continuity unconnected to developments in Virginia and Massachusetts. Native American people continued to build houses through the nineteenth century that were designed entirely on indigenous principles. Today in New Mexico and Arizona, many American Indian people live in houses that have nothing to do with their setting in the political entity of the United States. Throughout the nineteenth century, Hispanic architects in the rural Southwest built adobe homes of rooms strung in strings, bent around corners, and arranged along the sides of open courtyards. Their houses owed nothing to commotions in the world of the Anglos.

Another dramatic example is the shotgun house that John Vlach has studied so well. Developed in Haiti out of African and native forms, then brought to New Orleans, the shotgun house is an African-American contribution to the landscape. From Louisiana, the shotgun house diffused east and west, and it was carried against the grain of history, up the Mississippi and along the Ohio River, where it was adopted in the cities by new immigrants from Europe. A narrow run of rooms with a door in the gable end, the shotgun house breaks the American pattern in size and orientation. It is formally distinct, unrelated to the houses brought west from the Atlantic, but like the houses created in compromise, its entry is direct. Nothing architectural blocks your way in.

Native American and Hispanic people in the Southwest; African Americans in the Mississippi Valley; farming people in the

Southern Mountains, the southern Midwest, and the Deep South; Germans in Pennsylvania, Cajuns in Louisiana, Mormons in Utah — all connect in their reluctance to build baffles into their houses that would divide them from their neighbors. Join these objectively more sociable folks together, and they make a large minority of people who did not comply with the great change of the eighteenth century. If we bring the patterns together, all five of them, we will have gathered a clear majority of the houses of the nineteenth century, but I have not yet mentioned the pattern that dominates architectural histories of the period. Something is seriously wrong with research as it is conventionally practiced.

The sixth is the pattern of the books. In line with a developmental succession that began with the fashionable saltbox house, then proceeded to replace it with the Georgian house, designers in the nineteenth century looked around them, imagined improvements, and published books full of earnest advice. Some people followed their directions. They built the houses that historians use to divide the past into a neat series of periods, each one replacing the last on the track that leads to the present.

More of America's nineteenth-century designers created a seventh pattern. They selected ideas out of books, then they mixed them up and created a practice of accommodation and excitement. Their range of action was wide. At one extreme, prevalent from Pennsylvania and Virginia through the uplands of the South and West, the builders plucked a few ornamental details from the book and located them conventionally on the houses of continuity and compromise. At the other extreme, builders drew ideas from publications, blended them surprisingly, and invented synthetic new forms, especially in the era of the Greek Revival in upstate New York and the era of the Italianate in the Midwest and Deep South.

If we combine the pretentious, timid practice of the sixth pattern with the brave, innovative practice of the seventh pattern, we will not overbalance the view of the nineteenth century as a

Synthesis: Greek, Gothic, and Italianate. Bucksport, Maine. 1978

Accumulation: Greek with Italianate and Gothic additions.
Otsego County, New York. 1968

time dominated by different varieties of fluid, traditional practice that were aided rather than destroyed by new technologies. But the builders of the sixth and seventh patterns, though a minority, pointed the way to the future in the nineteenth century, just as the builders of the saltbox house, though a tiny minority in North America, did in their day. Early in the seventeenth century, architects in New England lit upon a modern form — symmetrical, closed, fragmented — that would not become general for nearly two centuries. During the nineteenth century, while others continued in the modern vein, or turned backward through the revival of open plans to premodern times, some architects established a postmodern practice. They accumulated commodities and arranged them to suit themselves.

Other options have not closed, but the twentieth century (a period that begins about 1920) is characterized by people who consume houses, reshape them through remodeling, and make them habitable through the organization of goods into domestic environments. People buy houses with an eye to their sale, and the home is less the house than it is a collection of portable furnishings that can be arranged familiarly in rented apartments, or in restored old houses, or in plastic-clad Queen Anne Revival-French Provincial mansions in the suburbs.

Pattern in Time

My argument is done. Architecture provides a prime resource to the one who would write a better history. I will contrive a conclusion with a summary. Our history breaks into three great periods. Its dynamic depends upon impurity.

First is the period of the village, a time of compressed housing and dispersed fields. The great creation of the period was the largest, most permanent, most lavishly adorned building of the community. Collective resources were banked and the collective will was materialized in a sacred edifice that was built to last, when houses were not. It should humble us some that the

Urnes stave church.
Sogn, Norway.
1995

San José. Trampas, New Mexico. 1987

religious buildings of this period are the world's greatest architectural creations: the parish churches of England, the stave churches of Norway, the earthen mosques of West Africa, the towering temples of India — Chartres Cathedral, the Selimiye at Edirne, the Todaiji at Nara.

In the beginning, there was the village, a neolithic invention, and in the beginning, there was enclosure. Valiant people carved farms out of the waste and built longhouses to shelter themselves and their stock against wolves and cattle raids. Enclosure expanded steadily, chewing away the wilderness on the margins, but it was blocked on the fat lowlands where enterprise was entangled in intricate webs of rights and obligations. Village people wanted to prosper, but no more than they wanted to live in confidence among their neighbors. Their cooperative arrangements worked economically, and their religion gave them a vision of unity. They wanted to prosper, but they understood that an appetite for worldly goods than ran beyond necessity was avarice — a sin as deadly as gluttony or fornication. The aim of life was sufficiently clarified by Christ's message that it is easier for a camel to go through the eye of a needle than it is for a rich man to enter the kingdom of God.

Still, as new routes to profit opened through international commerce, enclosure came down to the lowlands. Where men once plowed, sheep came to graze, growing wool for the merchants of the cities by the sea. Then pious reformers did to Christianity what the enclosers were doing to the landscape. They improved it through division, breaking it into pieces. With the religious disunion of the Reformation, greed was released, enclosure increased, and the saltbox house was invented.

The second period is the period of the house. The big buildings of the period were not religious but political. They were government cathedrals where secular power made its public display. They were factories where laws were manufactured to fill the void left by religion. In the United States, a dome was lifted from the religious tradition and set as a crown upon a bilaterally symmetrical, tripartite mass in Washington city. Smaller domes on state capitols, and still smaller domes on county courthouses, spread a network of civil command over the nation. The political buildings were big, but the great creation of the period was the family home.

In their asymmetry and openness, the first houses were fit to communal experience. They belonged to the period of the village. With enclosure, the house was broken out of the collective composition of the village. It came to stand apart — apart from other houses, and apart from the church. The church was disestablished on the enclosed landscape long before it was disestablished by law. As ownership of the land solidified, so did the house. It was rebuilt in permanent materials. Then, as though at last awakening to its aloneness, the house drew a cloak of symmetry over itself and, in hiding, commenced to subdivide its interior, transferring the class structures of the larger society into the little community of the family.

The new house centered the world. It stood away from the church and away from the barn in the midst of fields enclosed by fences. The capitol building of a miniature state, built upon the ruins of community, the house beamed a message of control and order over a shattered landscape. What builders created in houses, politicians then tried to create in society. But what builders created in houses was realized less effectively in politics than it was in technology. People expressed their desire for control and order through technical procedures, just as they did in the massing and ornamentation of geometric houses. At first with manual methods, and then with big machines, artisans made things in increasingly exact repetitious units and with increasingly smooth artificial surfaces.

When a closed house stood on an enclosed landscape, the modern age began. Local powers went down to defeat, while a new power expanded. Dedicated to material gain, protected by new laws and advanced by new machines, this new power signaled its victory in buildings composed of imported, industrial materials.

At the extreme limit of enclosure, the gargantuan pile of the country house stood on its estate, among gardens and parks, surrounded by high stone walls with spiky iron gates; down a lane ran rows of cottages where servants and agricultural laborers tried to live. Into the same position in the structure, next came the plantation with its big house and squalid quarters where human beings were held in captivity. Then it was the industrialist's mansion and a row of identical little dwellings for the mill hands. Putting the capital won from enclosure to work, the princes of industry built factories that served them as vast pastures and cotton fields had served others. They adopted and perfected the rational division of labor that was traditional to complex technologies. They appropriated the abundance of cheap labor that had been generated by the destruction of the villages. They exploited the disruption in family unity that was marked by the separation of the kitchen from the hall and the barn from the house.

No longer able to find good work in the countryside, laborers in need of cash left home. Daughters left the kitchen, fathers left the barn. They assembled in big buildings, filling slots in rigid, hierarchical schemes, and the factory produced great wealth for a few, and for the millions it made industrial commodities.

Third is the period of the commodity. The period's big building does not belong to religion or politics, but to business. At first, in a time of transition, it was the horizontal block of the factory, with its smooth brick walls, its endless rows of identical windows, its racket and smoke. Then it was a vertical marvel of engineering, a ludicrously phallic skyscraper where nothing was made.

As industrial capitalism expanded, some people continued to live in the period of the house. Others turned back toward the period of the village with new open homes. But slowly people came into conformity. They worked for wages, went shopping, and filled their houses with stuff. In this there was nothing new.

Industrial landscape. West Aliquippa, Pennsylvania. 1970

Archaeology teaches that people have always consumed commodities. Across the landscape of prehistoric Europe run the trade routes of the commerce in amber. A bibelot from India was found in the wreckage of Pompeii. Shards of pottery from England, Holland, and China are sifted out of the soil at American colonial sites. The difference is this: at one time, commodities made ornaments of peripheral importance in houses that people built to their own specifications with the help of their handy neighbors. But as industrialization continued, houses themselves became commodities, and people were assigned the difficult task of shaping their personalities out of things made by other people.

How people have handled their assignment is a topic of high importance. Happiness in this age depends in part on consumers finding ways to explore creativity and achieve humanity that are as fulfilling as the common work of the potter or farmer. Cooking might be one, gardening and decorating the home might be others. But there have been few studies of how individuals in the United States, at the beginning of the twenty-first century, compose commodities into expressions of their identities. There is not much evidence, so I speak as a cultural informant, and not as a student of culture, when I opine that the patterns of our time, hidden behind the walls of the house, are even more various and divergent than those of the nineteenth century. I end this little history with a call for research: in the coming years, the study of vernacular architecture should include patient ethnographic investigation of how commodities are assembled into domestic environments.

Three neat periods: if such a scheme is convincing at all, it is probably because it is, like the facade of the I-house, tripartite and bilaterally symmetrical. The front of the house has three parts, a middle one with a door, flanked by two with windows. My historical sketch also has three parts (village, house, commodity), just as ostensibly comprehensive accounts of society have three classes (upper, middle, lower). At the same time — the simultaneity of odd and even numbers being the key to its

I-house.
Page County,
Virginia.
1977

I-house.
Damascus, Maryland.
1969

I-house. Guernsey, Channel Islands. 1982

pretense to unity — the facade of the house is bilaterally symmetrical. A vertical line at the center will divide it into equal halves, and my triple pattern also divides into halves at industrialization in the middle of the middle period. I can speak at once of three periods and of preindustrial and industrial eras, just as we can divide the triple order of society into the halves of a professional class and a working class. Schemes that are simultaneously triple and double seem complete.

Insisting that the three periods are no more than a construction of convenience, I know that all histories are such constructions, and I believe my sketch could be elaborated into a history of the United States better than the one my daughter is taught in high school. But that is not my goal. Histories confined by national boundaries are, at best, transitional and fractional, pieces of the picture we need. What interests me is how architecture can help us puzzle the big picture together.

The three periods could aid in planning a program of research. With so many things available for study, it is wise to focus on the ones that are richest in significance. In medieval Europe, the object is the large and beautiful church. In America, between 1650 and 1920, the object is the house. In these late days, buildings are consumed by many but designed by few. Professional architects and professional planners have conspired with capitalists to steal from people their right to architectural design. Since people can be understood only from their own creations, from what they say and make, and not from what others say about them or make for them, our attention will concentrate on things smaller than churches or houses.

In the period of the commodity, we are reduced to transportable objects, charged with learning how they are made and marketed, how they are purchased and composed into displays within architectural spaces. Even the architect is less one who transforms nature than one who designs assemblies of prefabricated components. We are left with modification and pastiche. The image for our days is the old house remodeled, its interior a concatenation of commodities. Creation is restricted but not at an end. The potter still shapes the earth into pots. The householder receives ceramic pieces and arranges them on the dresser of her kitchen. Both create new entities, expressing themselves in art, making texts for us to interpret.

Our need is for a more expansive and inclusive history, one fit to the world we inhabit, a history that can guide improvements in architectural preservation and in new architectual design, a history that can help us in our effort to live meaningfully and decently upon the earth. It cannot be based solely on writing, the expressive mode of a rare few. Material culture — human work made permanent in buildings and books, in clothing and tools —provides the resource.

Selecting significant forms — the church, the house, the pot — is part of the job. Work has begun, and now the goal is to develop a method of comparison, free from mere chronology, that will help us understand general principles of historical action through the study of material culture. I have used architecture to illustrate how material culture can be read. Differences between local and imported materials, interiors and exteriors, massing and ornament, compression and dispersal at different levels of design — such distinctions prepare us for formal analysis, cultural interpretation, and historical comparison.

Historical comparison: when I came to the mountains of western Turkey in 1985, I found the people in the villages reorganizing their houses. During subsequent visits over a decade, I watched the process that people could tell me about in Ireland, that I had to dope out of analysis in Virginia.

When they were nomads, moving up to the high pastures in the summer and down to sheltered glens in the winter, the people built domed homes of felt stretched over staked frames. Settling permanently on the site of their winter encampment, they built houses of the same kind, with impaled frames and coats of felt. Once they were secure in their possession of the land, they rebuilt their houses in permanent materials. As in prehistoric

England and contemporary West Africa, round forms were squared off. The walls were built of heavy logs, notched at the corners, or more often of stone. The roofs were flat. They required constant maintenance, as thatching does in Ireland. After every rain, men went up to pack the earthen roofs with stone rollers. When it rained, the roof leaked, so the people borrowed ideas from the houses they saw in the towns where they sold their produce, their wheat and beans and carpets. A few houses with flat roofs remain, but now most houses have hipped roofs covered with purchased tiles.

With its walls of stone and its roof of tile, the house was permanent and snug. The exterior of the house was the outside of the inside. Doors gave direct access to the interior, where carpets covered the earthen floors, cushions were lined along the walls, and a fire flickered on the hearth.

Then, beginning in the 1960s, village people started to build houses with central hallways and bilaterally symmetrical facades, astonishingly like the I-houses of eighteenth-century Virginia. I asked why they were making the change. They said they wanted their houses to be cleaner. People in Ballymenone told me the same thing. But the answer only rearranges the question. In fact, their old houses were impeccably clean. Why did they suddenly think the house should be cleaner? They said that the new houses came with depopulation. People left for the cities, seeking jobs in factories. Those who stayed in the Turkish village were like those who survived the Famine in Ireland. A bad event had good results. The farmers who remained had more land. Expanding their agricultural holdings, they produced a surplus and accumulated wealth. Wealth brought goods — tractors, televisions, refrigerators — and differences of wealth disturbed communal unity. The wealthier people built bigger houses that symbolized their economic success, protected their belongings, and gave them, they said, more privacy.

Farmers in the mountains of western Turkey are in the middle of a change that Irish farmers remember. The old people in

New house. Çınarpınar, Çanakkale, Turkey. 1990

Village mosque. Çınarpınar, Çanakkale, Turkey. 1990

Ballymenone are balanced in their evaluation. The change, they say, was good for the family, but bad for the community. The young people in Ballymenone, knowing the old system only in its days of decline, think the change was nothing but good. Turkish farmers say that the community is less cohesive than it was, but life was too hard in the past. A little loss of social coherence is a small price to pay for the gain in comfort, and anyway, they say, the change has brought no serious rupture to the community. The person highest in status is not the one with the biggest house and the most goods. It is the woman who is the best weaver and teaches generously at the loom, it is the man who understands farming and leads the work in the fields, and above all, it is the person who is known to be a true Muslim.

Their houses are changing, but they live in a compact village. The houses stand close together. The fields are not enclosed; they expand into an unfenced patchwork of brilliant green. At harvest, teams of neighbors gather and reap the golden grain. Their cooperative economic arrangements are firm, and their faith is strong. Some of their new wealth goes into improving their homes, but even more conspicuously it is invested in the village mosque. Old mosques are being refurbished. Bright white new mosques are being built. And life is good, all praise to God.

Turkish farmers live simultaneously in the period of the village and the period of the house. Not really. They live in exactly the same time that you and I do, with as much right, and more capacity, to create the future. Predictions are only projections out of the few fragments of the present and past that chance to stick in the mind. No one knows whether their way or our way will prevail, but my prediction is that both will endure.

Out of my fieldwork, facts from Turkey come into association with facts from Ireland and America. Despite chronology, we see the similarities and the differences in historical action. Understanding expands. Facts combine to build the principles by which facts are interpreted. Facts do not dissipate into anecdotery. They become meaningful. As understanding increases, patterns at once clarify and complicate beyond all control. Any hope for evolutionary law — for a history of the world based on the history of the United States or England or France — dissolves in the empirical welter. History's big picture is a patterned picture of diversity.

Examined closely, analyzed formally on the ground of compassion, then manipulated into comparative arrangements, material culture breaks open to reveal the complexity of time, its simultaneous urges to progress, revitalization, and stability. The world's builders give us hope. Many routes lie open to the future.

Camelback shotgun. Louisville, Kentucky. 1994

Bergen, Norway. 1988

Log house. Nelson County, Virginia. 1977

ACKNOWLEDGMENTS

Behind the house, in decay, stood a log cabin. My grandmother's birthplace, it was built by her father after defeat in the Civil War. Her stories set the cabin in a time when important things still happened, though in my day it was home to the retired plowhorse I rode over the hills in boyish fantasy. My interests in architecture and history began there. In my grandfather's shop, I watched wood transform into fine pieces of furniture, learning the virtues of serious craft. What began with my grandparents was nurtured by my father when he returned from his war. It expanded when I went up to the Blue Ridge in search of ancient songs, and it was given professional form by Fred B. Kniffen. We met by chance, and listening to my enthusiastic talk about old barns and ballads, Mr. Kniffen said, "Lad, you could become the Francis James Child of folk architecture."

I have become no Child, but I learned well from Mr. Kniffen, sitting on a stool in his office at L.S.U. and looking at his photographs of American buildings. I followed his direction, believing, in the Boasian manner, that cultural creations recorded exactly in large numbers reveal patterns that contain the thinking of other people. Early in my career, in my continuing run of luck, I met James Marston Fitch. He invited me to Columbia for annual lectures on America's common buildings, and he shaped me into a preservationist. Next I met Jim Deetz to whom I am bound in fraternal affection. Our work has become twined into a joint effort of historical discovery based on anthropological precepts.

Those are the main ones who have made me. I have dedicated books to my grandparents and to my father, to Mr. Kniffen and Jim Deetz. This one is for James Marston Fitch, architect, preservationist, and architectural historian, who has given me hope by saying that that what has changed can change again.

My work has been aided and refined by my teachers in folklore, by Kenny Goldstein, by Bruce Buckley, Tris Coffin, and Don Yoder, and by generous colleagues in my discipline: Roger Abrahams, Ron Baker, İlhan Başgöz, Dick Bauman, John Burrison, Bob Cochran, Cece Conway, Linda Dégh, Dick Dorson, Alan Dundes, Bill Ferris, Bill Hansen, Lee Haring, Marjorie Hunt, Dell Hymes, Sandy Ives, Bill Ivey, Alan Jabbour, Kersti Jobs-Björklöf, Mike Jones, Suzi Jones, Charles Joyner, Shamsuzzaman Khan, Richard Kurin, Billy Lightfoot, Orvar Löfgren, John McDowell, Elliott Oring, Barry Lee Pearson, Phil Peek, Ralph Rinzler, Greg Schrempp, Pravina Shukla, Barre Toelken, Bill Wiggins, and Terry Zug.

I offer this book to my masters and friends in the movement for the study of vernacular architecture, among whom I must first name Fred Kniffen, and then Jim Deetz, Estyn Evans, James Marston Fitch, and Warren Roberts, and then these good colleagues: Jennifer Eastman Attebery, James Ayres, Alison Bell, Charles Bergengren, Hande Birkalan, Jean-Paul Bourdier, Peter Brink, Ronald Brunskill, Richard Candee, Tom Carter, Süheyla Çavuşer, Catherine Cresswell, Marsh Davis, Shannon

163

Docherty, Chip Frederick, Alan Gailey, Ritchie Garrison, Reha Günay, Bernie Herman, Tom Hubka, Jason Jackson, Sung-Kyun Kim, Peirce Lewis, Jiang Lu, Howard Marshall, Don McTernan, John Moe, Lyn Montell, Baqi'e Badawi Muhammad, Peter Nabokov, Paul Oliver, Jerry Pocius, Jules Prown, Bob St. George, Chris Sturbaum, Dell Upton, Camille Wells, Mats Widbom, Chris Wilson, John Vlach, and Wilbur Zelinsky.

John Gallman, director of the Indiana University Press, and a dear friend of mine, encouraged me to write a general book on material culture. John and his able staff—Jane Lyle, Susan Barnett, and Zig Zeigler—helped me get that work done. Then George Jevremović, the brother of my soul, suggested reworking the last chapter of *Material Culture* into this book, the second in the series co-published by the Indiana University Press and Material Culture of Philadelphia. Again, Michael Cavanagh and Kevin Montague printed my photographs, Kathy Foster and Karen Duffy read the text, John McGuigan wrestled the back matter onto disks, and Bruce Carpenter, using the sketches I made of every page, composed the book for the computer.

At last, I am sustained in my work by the circle of friends around me: Saki Bercovitch, Bruce and Inta Carpenter, Karen Duffy, Tom and Ellen Ehrlich, İbrahim and Ayşe Erdeyer, Marshall Fishwick, Allen and Polly Grimshaw, Mehmet and Tülay Gürsoy, Bill and Mary Beth Hansen, Lee Haring, George Jevremović, David Logan and Dale Hodges, Firoz and Daisy Mahmud, John McDowell and Pat Glushko, John McGuigan, John and Mona Pearson, Shaheen and Salma Rahman, Ahmet and Nurten Şahin, Mohammad Ayub and Fouzia Salahuddin, Greg Schrempp, Pravina Shukla, Kemal and June Sılay, and Takashi Takahara.

Most of all, I am grateful to my family, to Wally and Isabella, Judy and Bill, Polly, Harry and Lori, Lydia and Tom, and to Kathy and Ellen Adair, who make our old wooden house on the west side of town a place of love.

NOTES

P. 17. Toward the beginning of this essay, a few fragments survive from a talk I gave at a conference on vernacular architecture at the Middle East Technical University in Ankara, Turkey, in 1982. That talk was printed as "Vernacular Architecture and Society," *Material Culture* 16:1 (1984): 4–24, and it has been reprinted in: Simon J. Bronner, ed., *American Material Culture and Folklife: A Prologue and Dialogue* (Ann Arbor: UMI Research Press, 1985), pp. 47–62; Daniel W. Ingersoll, Jr. and Gordon Bronitsky, eds. *Mirror and Metaphor: Material and Social Constructions of Reality* (Lanham: University Press of America, 1987), pp. 229–45; Mete Turan, ed., *Vernacular Architecture: Paradigms of Environmental Response* (Aldershot: Avebury, 1990), pp. 271–84; and *Traditional Dwellings and Settlements Review* 1:2 (1990): 9–21. This essay starts where the old one did, then it goes in directions that would have been impossible for me in 1982, when my fieldwork had been limited to the eastern United States, Britain, and Ireland.

P. 21. Another reason for architectural history following art history is provided by Dell Upton in *Architecture in the United States* (Oxford: Oxford University Press, 1998), pp. 262–72, when he describes architects, insecure in their identity and wishing to separate themselves from builders, adopting the pose of the artist. One consequence of their pose is a restriction in the use of the professional title. Whether or not they were trained professionally, painters are painters, poets are poets, but some writers call designers of buildings architects only if they were educated and licensed in a particular way. The greatest poets—Homer, Shakespeare—were not trained in the university, and there is no good reason why designers of cathedrals or chicken coops, though not trained in the university, should not be called architects.

P. 25. I tell about the change in roofing in *Passing the Time in Ballymenone: Culture and History of an Ulster Community* (Philadelphia: University of Pennsylvania Press, 1982; Bloomington: Indiana University Press, 1995), pp. 414–22; *Turkish Traditional Art Today* (Bloomington: Indiana University Press, 1993), pp. 261, 635; and *Art and Life in Bangladesh* (Bloomington: Indiana University Press, 1997), pp. 254–55. The pattern I found in Turkey is also found in the Southwest: Nancy Hunter Warren, *Villages of Hispanic New Mexico* (Santa Fe: School of American Research Press, 1987), chapter 4; Charles L. Briggs, *Competence in Performance: The Creativity of Tradition in Mexicano Verbal Art* (Philadelphia: University of Pennsylvania Press, 1988), p. 77.

P. 29. Åke Campbell's attractive evaluation has often been repeated, for example in the excellent *Atlas of the Irish Rural Landscape* (Cork: Cork University Press, 1997), p. 147, edited by F. H. A. Aalen, Kevin Whelan, and Matthew Stout. In his first report of the five weeks he spent in fieldwork in 1934, "Irish Fields and Houses: A Study of Rural Culture," *Béaloideas* 5:1 (1935): 57–74, Campbell described a farm in Kerry and offered a series of highly important observations, connecting Ireland to the highland pastoral tradition, and noting two basic house types, one with the chimney on the gable, the other with the chimney set cen-

165

trally, and he generalized (p. 58): "The humanizing of the landscape has developed until the natural landscape is now almost wholly defaced."

Pp. 32–34. The log cabin is so important to American views of the self that scholars have lost their cool in arguments over its origins. The main old texts are: Henry C. Mercer, *The Origin of Log Houses in the United States* (Doylestown: Bucks County Historical Society, 1976, pub. 1924) and Harold R. Shurtleff, *The Log Cabin Myth* (Gloucester: Peter Smith, 1967, pub. 1939). Fred Kniffen allowed me to co-author with him the paper that summed things up in the sixties: "Building in Wood in the Eastern United States: A Time-Place Perspective," *The Geographical Review* 56:1 (1966): 40–66, reprinted in Dell Upton and John Michael Vlach, eds., *Common Places: Readings in American Vernacular Architecture* (Athens: University of Georgia Press, 1986), pp. 159–81. I still believe that I got the story about right in my first paper, published when I was still an undergraduate: "The Appalachian Log Cabin," *Mountain Life and Work* 39:4 (1963): 5–14, reprinted in: W. K. McNeil, ed., *Appalachian Images in Folk and Popular Culture* (Ann Arbor: UMI Research Press, 1989), pp. 307–14; and George O. Carney, ed., *Baseball, Barns, and Bluegrass: A Geography of American Folklife* (Lanham: Rowman and Littlefield, 1998), pp. 19–28. That old paper was much refined as "The Types of the Southern Mountain Cabin," in Jan H. Brunvand, *The Study of American Folklore* (New York: W.W. Norton, 1968), pp. 338–70. Horizontal log construction was brought by many different groups to North America, but the variety that became dominant on the eastern frontier was that of the Pennsylvania Germans, though modi-

fied through synthesis with techniques from English framing. Since there is no necessary connection in origin between technology and form, the most usual form of the log cabin was not German, but English or Irish. Among the many good regional studies of American log buildings are these: Terry G. Jordan, *Texas Log Buildings: A Folk Architecture* (Austin: University of Texas Press, 1978); Warren E. Roberts, *Log Buildings in Southern Indiana* (Bloomington: Trickster Press, 1996, pub. 1984); Donald A. Hutslar, *Log Construction in the Ohio Country, 1750–1850* (Athens: Ohio University Press, 1992); John Morgan, *The Log House in East Tennessee* (Knoxville: University of Tennessee Press, 1990); Charles E. Martin, *Hollybush: Folk Building and Social Change in an Appalachian Community* (Knoxville: University of Tennessee Press, 1984), chapters 2–3; and Jennifer Eastman Attebery, *Building with Logs: Western Log Construction in Context* (Moscow: University of Idaho Press, 1998).

P. 36. I expand upon the way in which cosmological presuppositions condition action upon the world in "Nature, Culture, and Cosmological Interference," a paper presented at a congress of the Deutsche Gesellschaft für Volkskunde, slated for publication in the society's proceedings for the year 2000.

P. 37. The double-crib barn is type B in Charles H. Dornbusch and John K. Heyl, *Pennsylvania German Barns* (Allentown: Schlechter's, 1958). I described the southern extension of the form in "The Pennsylvania Barn in the South: Part I," *Pennsylvania Folklife* 15:2 (1965/66): 8–19; and I did a better job with it in "The Double-Crib Barn in South-Central Pennsylvania," *Pioneer America* 1:1 (1969): 9–16; 1:2 (1969):

40–45; 2:1 (1970): 47–52; 2:2 (1970): 23–34. In his good book *The Pennsylvania Barn: Its Origin, Evolution, and Distribution in North America* (Baltimore: Johns Hopkins University Press, 1992), Robert F. Ensminger does not treat the double-crib barn, which is unfortunate because it holds the key to much of the formal development of the large banked barns of Pennsylvania. An elaboration of the double-crib form is documented by Marian Moffett and Lawrence Wodehouse in *East Tennessee Cantilever Barns* (Knoxville: University of Tennessee Press, 1993). The common transverse-crib barn was a transformation of the double-crib: Henry Glassie, *Pattern in the Material Folk Culture of the Eastern United States*, (Philadelphia: University of Pennsylvania Press, 1969), pp. 88–99; Terry G. Jordan-Bychkov, "Transverse-Crib Barns, The Upland South, and Pennsylvania Extended," *Material Culture* 30:2 (1998): 5–31.

Pp. 39. In his excellent book on traditional pottery in Georgia, *Brothers in Clay: The Story of Georgia Folk Pottery* (Athens: University of Georgia Press, 1983), p. 9, John Burrison comments that the one-man shop was not the norm in the past; it is a twentieth-century expedient. On the traditionality of divisions in labor, see Henry Glassie, *Material Culture* (Bloomington: Indiana University Press, 1999), pp. 51–53, 175–78, 200–205.

Pp. 39–40. I have never published the results of our work in Greene County, but a full report, "Architecture in Log in Southwestern Pennsylvania," was submitted to the Information Office of Northern Ireland in 1973, and it became the basis for architectural replication at the Ulster-American Folk Park, Camphill, Omagh, County Tyrone, Northern Ireland.

P. 40. John James, *Chartres: The Masons Who Built a Legend* (London: Routledge and Kegan Paul, 1982).

P. 40. Warren Roberts, "The Tools Used in Building Log Houses in Indiana," in Upton and Vlach, *Common Places*, pp. 182–203.

Pp. 41–43. I describe Paddy McBrien's house in *Passing the Time in Ballymenone*, pp. 387, 412–13.

Pp. 44–45. Karagömlek's new mosques: Glassie, *Turkish Traditional Art Today*, pp. 742–46.

P. 45. A builder in Ethiopia said that architectural plans are only for people who don't know what they are doing: Naigzy Gebremedhin, "Some Traditional Types of Housing in Ethiopia," in Paul Oliver, ed., *Shelter in Africa* (New York: Praeger, 1971), p. 120.

Pp. 45–46. For Haripada Pal, see Glassie, *Art and Life in Bangladesh*, chapter 6.

P. 52. For the yurt: Svat Soucek, "The Yurt in Inner Asia, and Yurts in Turkey: Some General As Well As Specific Observations," in Sabri M. Akural, ed., *Turkic Culture: Continuity and Change* (Bloomington: Turkish Studies, 1987), pp. 171–78; Johannes Kalter, *The Arts and Crafts of Turkestan* (London: Thames and Hudson, 1984), pp. 43–51. The tipi: Robert H. Lowie, *The Crow Indians* (New York: Holt, Rinehart and Winston, 1956, pub. 1935), pp. 86–92; Royal B. Hassrick, *The Sioux: Life and Customs of a Warrior Society* (Norman: University of Oklahoma Press, 1964), pp. 210–15, 235–37.

Pp. 52–55. The Wealden house: M. W. Barley, *The English Farmhouse and Cottage* (London: Routledge and Kegan Paul, 1961), pp.26–30; Eric Mercer, *English Vernacular Houses* (London: Royal Commission on Historical Monuments, 1975), pp. 11–14; Richard Harris, *Discovering Timber-Framed Buildings* (Aylesbury: Shire, 1978), pp. 65–67; R. W. Brunskill, *Houses* (London: Collins, 1982), pp. 58–61; R. T. Mason, *Framed Buildings of the Weald* (Horsham: Coach, 1969), chapters 2–3; and Anthony Quiney, *Kent Houses* (Woodbridge: Antique Collectors' Club, 1993), pp. 137–56.

Pp. 61–65. Mrs. Cutler's kitchen is the prime text of chapter 13 in my *Passing the Time in Ballymenone,* and I feature Gökyurt in the chapter on vernacular architecture in *Turkish Traditional Art Today,* pp. 264–71. For more on the Irish dresser, see Claudia Kinmonth, *Irish Country Furniture: 1700–1959* (New Haven: Yale University Press, 1993), chapter 3.

P. 66. Dell Upton describes the search for women in architecture in *Architecture in the United States,* pp. 272–79. William Morris, *News from Nowhere; or, an Epoch of Rest, Being Some Chapters from a Utopian Romance* (Hammersmith: Kelmscott Press, 1892), chapter 26. In chapter 15, on work, art, and the kind of commercial colonialism that is called globalization today, William Morris makes a concise presentation of the essentials of his thinking.

P. 66. My generalization on North America comes straight from this excellent book: Peter Nabokov and Robert Easton, *Native American Architecture* (New York: Oxford University Press, 1989), p. 30. For women as builders in Africa: Susan Denyer, *African Traditional Architecture* (New York: Africana, 1978), p. 92; Labelle Prussin, *Architecture in Northern Ghana* (Berkeley: University of California Press, 1969), pp. 57–58, 97; Jean-Paul Bourdier and Trinh T. Minh-ha, *African Spaces: Designs for Living in Upper Volta* (New York: Africana, 1985), pp. 45, 47, 105–6, 162–63; T. C. Anyamba and A. A. Adebaye, *Traditional Architecture: Settlement, Evolution and Built Form* (Nairobi: Jomo Kenyatta Foundation, 1993), p. 20; and Franco Frescura, *Rural Shelter in Southern Africa* (Johannesburg: Ravan Press, 1981), p. 14.

P. 67. See James Deetz, *Flowerdew Hundred: The Archaeology of a Virginia Plantation, 1619–1864* (Charlottesville: University Press of Virginia, 1993), pp. 124–32.

P. 69. See: Marian Wenzel, *House Decoration in Nubia* (London: Duckworth, 1972); Stella Kramrisch, *The Hindu Temple,* 2 vols. (Delhi: Motilal Banarsidass, 1996, pub. 1946).

P. 69. My reference is to the passage on ornament in the chapter "The Lamp of Beauty," in John Ruskin's *The Seven Lamps of Architecture* (Sunnyside: George Allen, 1883, pub.1849), especially pp. 135–36.

Pp. 71–74. Talbot Hamlin's *Greek Revival Architecture: Being an Account of Important Trends in American Architecture and American Life Prior to the War Between the States* (New York: Dover, 1964, pub. 1944) introduces the style without attending to formal transformations, leaving a wonderful topic for one who would settle into the analysis of the houses of the period in New York, Ohio, and Michigan. Examples can be found in Richard N. Campen, *Architecture of the Western Reserve, 1800–1900* (Cleveland: Press of Case Western Reserve University, 1971). Fred

W. Peterson analyzes the western single-wing variety of the Greek Revival form in his good book *Homes in the Heartland: Balloon Frame Farmhouses of the Upper Midwest, 1850–1900* (Lawrence: University of Kansas Press, 1992), chapter 5.

P. 76. In *American Architecture Since 1780: A Guide to the Styles* (Cambridge: The MIT Press, 1969), Marcus Whiffen presents the sequence of styles clearly. The problem is that very few houses fit the sequence neatly.

Pp. 79–82. I describe the architecture of Bangladesh in the first chapter *of Art and Life in Bangladesh*. See also: A. K. M. Islam, *A Bangladesh Village: Political Conflict and Cohesion* (Prospect Heights: Waveland Press, 1987, pub. 1974), pp. 44–48, 55–58, 61, 67–68; Khondkar Iftekhar Ahmed, *Up to the Waist in Mud: Earth-Based Architecture in Rural Bangladesh* (Dhaka: University Press, 1994), pp. 6–15, 25–31, 43–44, 47–48, 94–95, 105, 107, 112, 115, 118; Syed Mahmudul Hasan, "Folk Architecture of Bangladesh," in Shamsuzzaman Khan, ed., *Folklore of Bangladesh* (Dhaka: Bangla Academy, 1987), pp. 424–45; and Saif-ul-Haq, "Architecture within the Folk Tradition: A Representation from Bangladesh," *Traditional Dwellings and Settlements Review* 5:2 (1994): 61–72.

Pp. 82–85. As is the case throughout this book, the information from Sweden is based on my own fieldwork, but I know Sweden less well than I do Bangladesh (or Ireland or Turkey) and I wish to acknowledge the help of good friends: Kersti Jobs-Björklöf, Mats Widbom, and Christer Ekelund. Two excellent publications deal with the villages I visited: Roland Andersson, *Byar och Färbodar i Leksands Kommun: Kulturhistorisk Mil-*

jönalys (Leksand: Dalarna Museum, 1983) and Lillie Hågglund, *Bilder Från Ullvi by* (Leksand: Leksands Kommun, 1983). The great text, a monument of vernacular architecture study, is Sigurd Erixon, *Svensk Byggnadskultur* (Stockholm: Aktiebolaget Bokverk, 1947); see especially pp. 286–346, 641–717. And I was aided by the excellent report, "The Dwelling as a Cultural Phenomenon," submitted by Christer Ekelund and Mats Widbom to the Swedish Council for Building Research in December 1988.

Pp. 85–87. For the longhouse, see Mercer, *English Vernacular Houses*, chapter 3. W. G. Hoskins describes the longhouses of Devon in the first chapter of *Old Devon* (London: Pan Books, 1966). The architecture of Wales has been studied magnificently. For the Welsh longhouse, see these important works: Iorwerth C. Peate, *The Welsh House: A Study in Folk Culture* (London: The Honourable Society of Cymmrodorion, 1940), chapter 4; Sir Cyril Fox and Lord Raglan, *Monmouthshire Houses* (Cardiff: National Museum of Wales, 1951–1954), I, pp. 88–90; II, pp. 104–8; III, pp. 82–85; S. R. Jones and J. T. Smith, "The Houses of Breconshire," *Brycheinog* 9 (1963): 5–34; 11 (1965): 50–89; 12 (1966/67): 23–53; and Peter Smith, *Houses of the Welsh Countryside: A Study in Historical Geography* (London: Royal Commission on Ancient and Historical Monuments in Wales, 1988), chapters 4, 9, 10. I report the seventeenth-century sources for Ireland in *Passing the Time in Ballymenone*, pp. 376–79, and describe the linear farm plan on pp. 343–51.

91. D. W. Meinig closes the important book he edited on *The Interpretation of Ordinary Landscapes* (New York: Oxford University Press, 1979) with an essay on the contributions of W. G. Hoskins and J. B. Jackson, two of the most influential of the scholars of the landscape. Jackson is of great importance in the United States; see his *Discovering the Vernacular Landscape* (New Haven: Yale University Press, 1984). Because, as Meinig points out (pp. 203, 229), Hoskins believed above all in the facts, while Jackson proceeds by argument, offering little by way of documentation or demonstration, I would have paired Hoskins with Fred Kniffen if I needed an American master, and I believe the best pairing would be W. G. Hoskins and E. Estyn Evans. Both authored a grand statement: Hoskins, *The Making of the English Landscape* (London: Hodder and Stoughton, 1955); Evans, *The Personality of Ireland: Habitat, Heritage and History* (Cambridge: University Press, 1973). Both wrote a superb local study: Hoskins, *The Midland Peasant: The Economic and Social History of a Leicestershire Village* (London: Macmillan, 1965); Evans, *Mourne Country: Landscape and Life in South Down* (Dundalk: Dundalgan Press, 1967). Both wrote popular accounts of regions: Hoskins, *Midland England: A Survey of the Country between the Chilterns and the Trent* (London: B. T. Batsford, 1949) and *Devon* (London: Collins, 1954); Evans, *Northern Ireland* (London: Collins, 1951). Both concentrated on the rural, for most of the landscape is rural, but both wrote on cities: Hoskins, *Two Thousand Years in Exeter* (Exeter: James Townsend, 1960); Evans, ed., *Belfast in Its Regional Setting: A Scientific Survey* (Belfast: British Association for the Advancement of Science, 1952). For both there are major collections of essays: Hoskins, *Provincial England: Essays in Social and Economic History* (London: Macmillan, 1965); Evans, *Ireland and the Atlantic Heritage: Selected Writings* (Dublin: Lilliput Press, 1996).

Both of these men wrote elegantly and passionately; both were impatient with the impatience of the twentieth century, and while Meinig is right to fault Hoskins for his lack of interest in modern phenomena (pp. 206–9), the intensity of his belief not only led Hoskins to write clearly, it led him to use modern technology to reach a wider audience. The books Hoskins wrote to accompany his television work are exemplary popular presentations of important ideas: *English Landscapes* (London: British Broadcasting Corporation, 1973) and *One Man's England* (London: British Broadcasting Corporation, 1978). Evans used lectures, the radio, and the museum to get his ideas to the public; he was instrumental in founding the Ulster Folk and Transport Museum, one of the very best outdoor museums in the world. Hoskins is, at last, a historian, and he prepared two important guides for local historical research: *Local History in England* (London: Longmans, Green, 1959) and *Fieldwork in Local History* (London: Faber and Faber, 1969). Evans is, at last, a social scientist, a geographer, archaeologist, and ethnologist. He wrote a major statement on Irish archaeology in *Prehistoric and Early Christian Ireland: A Guide* (London: B. T. Batsford, 1966). He wrote two important books on Irish folk culture: *Irish Heritage: The Landscape, The People and Their Work* (Dundalk: W. Tempest, 1963, pub. 1942) and *Irish Folk Ways* (New York: Devin-Adair, 1957). And Evans did not limit himself to Ireland; he wrote *France: A Geographical Introduction* (London: Christophers, 1951, pub. 1937). W. G. Hoskins and E. Estyn Evans both inspired a host of followers who work productively along the trails they blazed. Together they show how exacting study in the field and clear, passionate exposition can bring humanistic and social scientific concerns and methods into unity. Their works best exemplify the hope for historical study in material culture.

Pp. 91–92. The idea of two zones is too simple: Hoskins, *Making of the English Landscape*, p. 38. The village landscape of Japan is described well by Tsuneo Sato, "Tokugawa Villages and Agriculture," in Chie Nakane, Shinzaburo Oishi, and Conrad Totman, eds., *Tokugawa Japan: The Social and Economic Antecedents of Modern Japan* (Tokyo: University of Tokyo Press, 1991), pp. 37–80.

Pp. 92–94. I describe the Turkish village in *Turkish Traditional Art Today*, chapter 9. The architecture and dispersed settlement of the eastern Black Sea region are presented by Orhan Özgüner in *Köyde Mimari: Doğu Karadeniz* (Ankara: Orta Doğu Teknik Üniversitesi Mimarlık Fakültesi, 1970). The Irish system of rundale is described by E. Estyn Evans in *Irish Folk Ways*, pp. 20–26, 32–34, and in his introduction to the facsimile reprint of the fifth edition (1889) of Lord George Hill's *Facts from Gweedore* (Belfast: Institute of Irish Studies, 1971). Rundale—the Irish openfield system—is also described by F. H. A. Aalen in his excellent book *Man and the Landscape in Ireland* (London: Academic Press, 1978), pp. 181–87, 220–25.

P. 94. Lowry Nelson provides a fine account in *The Mormon Village: A Pattern and Technique of Land Settlement* (Salt Lake City: University of Utah Press, 1952). Thomas Carter describes Mormon houses excellently in his paper "Folk Design in Utah Architecture, 1849–1890," in the book he edited, *Images of an American Land: Vernacular Architecture in the Western United States* (Albuquerque: University of New Mexico Press, 1997), pp. 41–60. And see Thomas Carter and Julie Osborne, *A Way of Seeing: Discovering the Art of Building in Spring City, Utah* (Salt Lake City: Graduate School of Architecture, University of Utah, 1994).

P. 96. The story of the English village and its enclosure is told by W. G. Hoskins in *Making of the English Landscape*, chapters 2–6. The topic has a vast, complicated, and contentious bibliography, but one clear history is W. E. Tate's *The Enclosure Movement* (New York: Walker and Company, 1967). The movement divides into three great phases: thirteenth to fifteenth centuries, sixteenth and seventeenth, eighteenth and nineteenth. The last, the period of parliamentary enclosure, was marked by a diminishing of argument (Tate, p. 86) but the middle period, most important for America, inspired outrage among intellectuals, like Sir Thomas More, and it drove the peasants to rebellious action; it was the time of the Levellers and the Diggers. Through its long history, the argument for enclosure was that it promoted agricultural improvement and increased profits. The argument against enclosure was that it led to depopulation of the land and to misery for the poor. But the poor were called lazy, their communal culture stood in the way of progress, and enclosure triumphed despite the opposition of Christian moralists. The issues and results are about the same in the United States when poor people are removed from their neighborhoods in the cities by urban renewal or driven from their family farms when their land is taken and made into parks for the pleasure of the prosperous. The spirit of enclosure—progressive, profiteering, and disdainful of poor people and local cultures—continues. Tate ends his calm, balanced history by seeing the enclosure movement as an economic success and a social disaster (p. 175).

P. 107. W. G. Hoskins, *Making of the English Landscape*, pp. 138–39. For a little on Braunton: Roy Millward and Adrian Robinson, *North Devon and North Cornwall* (London: Macmillan Education, 1971), pp. 73–79; A. H. Slee, *Victorian Days in a Devon Village* (Braunton: S. J. H. Slee, 1978), chapters 1–2.

P. 112. For the New England landscape, see these general statements: John R. Stilgoe, *Common Landscape of America, 1580 to 1845* (New Haven: Yale University Press, 1982), pp. 17–18, 43–58; D. W. Meinig, *The Shaping of America: A Geographical Perspective on 500 Years of History* (New Haven: Yale University Press, 1986), I, pp. 91–109, 243–44, 413–14; and David Hackett Fischer, *Albion's Seed: Four British Folkways in America* (New York: Oxford University Press, 1989), pp. 181–205. And these excellent studies: Sumner Chilton Powell, *Puritan Village: The Formation of a New England Town* (Middletown Wesleyan University Press, 1970, pub. 1963); and J. Ritchie Garrison, *Landscape and Material Life in Franklin County, Massachusetts, 1770–1860* (Knoxville: University of Tennessee Press, 1991), chapter 2.

Pp. 114–16. Tax records: A. L. Shoemaker, ed., *The Pennsylvania Barn* (Kutstown: Pennsylvania Folklife Society, 1959), p. 9. I describe the Pennsylvania farm plan in "Eighteenth-Century Cultural Process in Delaware Valley Folk Building," *Winterthur Portfolio* 7 (1972): 29–57, reprinted in Upton and Vlach, *Common Places*, pp. 394–425. Unified German buildings in the United States: Richard W. E. Perrin, *Historic Wisconsin Buildings: A Survey of Pioneer Architecture, 1835–1870* (Milwaukee: Milwaukee Public Museum, 1962), pp. 14–25; Charles van Ravenswaay, *The Arts and Architecture of German Settlements in Missouri* (Columbia: University of Missouri Press, 1977), pp. 266–67, 279–84.

P. 116. Thomas C. Hubka, *Big House, Little House, Back House, Barn: The Connected Farm Buildings of New England* (Hanover: University Press of New England, 1984). The pattern that Hubka discovered—of farm buildings becoming more unified in the nineteenth century—I had noted in the study of one farm in upstate New York and reported in a paper which, though early and rough, I thought would become a model for fieldwork in its consideration of the whole farm as a unit (as opposed to the focus on building types), and in its blending of oral history, architectural history, and agricultural history; see "The Wedderspoon Farm," *New York Folklore Quarterly* 22:3 (1966): 165–87. But that did not become the norm for research, and it was Tom Hubka who brought the idea to fruition in his excellent book. Now it should be the model for the future.

Pp. 116–17. I reported my work in *Folk Housing in Middle Virginia: A Structural Analysis of Historic Artifacts* (Knoxville: University of Tennessee Press, 1976). Generally criticisms of that book have struck me as irrelevant, but in *Housing Culture: Traditional Architecture in an English Landscape* (London: UCL Press, 1993), p. 36, Matthew Johnson is quite right when he says the grammar of building is "unnecessarily cumbersome," and, in retrospect, I had come to his conclusion that constructing two models of competence would have been rhetorically preferable; at the same time, I could not have comprehended the nature of the duality until I had schematized the unity, and the complex conceptualization helped me understand change: in the transitional moment, the builder's competence, simultaneously incorporating two processes of design, was a bit cumbersome. Dell Upton illustrates how a better historian would have handled comparable data in "Vernacular Domestic Architecture in Eighteenth-Century Virginia," in Upton and Vlach, *Common Places*, pp. 315–35. In *The Transformation of Virginia: 1740–1790* (New York: W. W. Norton, 1988, pub. 1982), Rhys Isaac marvelously enriched our understanding of the period of architectural change. Using written sources and making them yield hints about life beyond the world of rich white men, Isaac reveals the political, religious, and especially the religious-political tensions of the period, confirming and deepening the notion of images of order that compensate for disorder on a dispersed landscape; see pp. 30–38, 51–59, 70–81, 116–20, 131–35, 147–77, 183, 197–98, 276, 292–95, 302–6, 310–12, 320–22, 327, 354–55. But nothing basic has been unsettled by later research, and the wonder to me is how close I came, with little time and no money, when I was twenty-five. For more on the architecture of the region: Marcus Whiffen, *The Eighteenth-Century Houses of Williamsburg* (Williamsburg: Colonial Williamsburg Foundation, 1985, pub. 1960); and Henry Chandlee Forman, *The Architecture of the Old South: The Medieval Style, 1585–1850* (Cambridge: Harvard University Press, 1948).

P. 117. The classic statement on the I-house is Fred Kniffen's article "Folk Housing: Key to Diffusion," appropriately taken from *Annals of the Association of American Geographers* 55:4 (1965): 459–77, and reprinted as the first paper in Upton and Vlach, *Common Places*, pp. 3–26. Mr. Kniffen had been using the term for a long time when he wrote that paper; it appears in the article with which, for me, the modern study of American vernacular architecture begins: "Louisiana House Types," *Annals of the Association of American Geographers* 26 (1936): 179–93, reprinted in Philip L. Wagner and Marvin W. Mikesell, eds., *Readings in Cultural Geography* (Chicago: University of Chicago Press, 1962), pp. 157–69.

P. 117. James Deetz argues effectively and correctly against the simplistic notion of "power relations" that replaces analysis in many writings about architecture; see *Flowerdew Hundred*, p. 65.

P. 121. For the change in English houses that took place between 1570 and 1640, before the English Revolution, see the notes to p. 138 below.

P. 122. To say that the climate conditioned the choice of dwelling in New England and Virginia is to state the obvious. James Marston Fitch has written a great book on the environmental influences upon design in *American Building 2: The Environmental Forces That Shape It* (Boston: Houghton Mifflin, 1972). In his earlier book *American Building: The Forces That Shape It* (Boston: Houghton Mifflin, 1948), pp. 10–14, Fitch began by noting the need in New England for heat and in the South for ventilation. Houses were not invented to fulfill those needs, but the houses that were selected from the large English repertory did provide heat in the North and ventilation in the South. Yet, to his excellent study of Virginia's houses in the period of diversity that precedes the period of conformity in every American region, Fraser D. Neiman appends a footnote, declaring consideration of climatic conditions, during explanation of architectural differences between New England and Virginia, to be "environmental determinism at its worst." It is not environmental determinism to consider the climate as an influence on design. Neiman argues further that the environmental rationale for the positioning of chimneys in the South makes no sense because people had separate kitchens. Many houses did not have separate kitchens. Even if they did, there is no basis for assuming that small meals were not prepared in the main house. In my time in Virginia, I never heard anyone use the word "hall" for the room that scholars call a hall. I did, however, hear it called "the fireplace room," and I was told that a fire was kept going in it in all weathers (exactly as in Ireland and in other parts of the South) so visitors could be entertained immediately. But even if the chimney were cold, its position centrally behind a central door would block the flow of air; the location of chimneys in the South seems to have less to do with the creation of heat than with the creation of passages for wind. If we were allowed only one explanation for architectural design, I would prefer a social explanation to an environmental one. The shift from one monofunctional argument to another is progress: we move from the climate to tradition to social status, and things seem to be going forward. But real advancement would be marked by a shift from single causes to multiple causes, and it is

necessary to consider the environment among them. I go on like this because Neiman's paper, "Domestic Architecture at the Clifts Plantation: The Social Context of Early Virginia Building," was reprinted (pp. 292–314) in the most important book on American vernacular architecture, *Common Places* by Upton and Vlach, and because his opinion was repeated by James Deetz in his book, the best of books on American material culture, *In Small Things Forgotten: An Archaeology of Early American Life* (New York: Anchor Books, 1996, pub. 1977), p. 153.

Pp. 122–26. The houses of southeastern England are described in P. Eden, "Smaller Post-medieval Houses in Eastern England," in Lionel Munby, ed., *East Anglian Studies* (Cambridge: W. Heffer, 1968), pp. 71–93. Eden's class J is the usual southeastern type; his class L moves the service to the rear, enabling a symmetrical facade, but it is far less common in England than it is in New England. It is not hard for the American in search of antecedents to find saltbox houses in England, but they are not easily found in the literature, since English authors are correctly concerned with the statistically dominant forms. Harry Forrester does show both the common asymmetrical form and the rarer saltbox form in *The Timber-Framed Houses of Essex: A Short Review of Their Types and Details, 14th to 18th Centuries* (Chelmsford: Tindal Press, 1959), pp. 14–20. There is an excellent bibliography on early New England houses: J. Frederick Kelly, *The Early Domestic Architecture of Connecticut* (New Haven: Yale University Press, 1924); Anthony N. B. Garvan, *Architecture and Town Planning in Colonial Connecticut* (New Haven:

Yale University Press, 1951); Clay Lancaster, *The Architecture of Historic Nantucket* (New York: McGraw-Hill, 1972); Abbott Lowell Cummings, *The Framed Houses of Massachusetts Bay, 1625–1725* (Cambridge: Harvard University Press, 1979). The best introduction, I believe, to early New England architecture is Robert Blair St. George, "'Set Thine House in Order': The Domestication of the Yeomanry in Seventeenth-Century New England," in Jonathan L. Fairbanks and Robert F. Trent, eds., *New England Begins: The Seventeenth Century* (Boston: Museum of Fine Arts, 1982), II, pp. 159–351, revised in Upton and Vlach, *Common Places*, pp. 336–64.

P. 126. See Dana Arnold, ed., *The Georgian Villa* (Phoenix Mill: Alan Sutton, 1996).

P. 129. The central hallway and symmetrical facade clearly indicate the presence of the Georgian idea in the largest houses. Its presence in the smallest houses is much subtler. The early form of the small house is like the cabin I illustrated on pp. 84–85 of *Folk Housing in Middle Virginia*: the door is set near the center of the front; the plan, while squarish, might be rectangular, and the house might be partitioned internally into a large room and a small one, like a tiny hall-and-parlor house. The later cabin, about the same in size, has the door set far to one end of the front, away from the chimney; the plan is square and generally unpartitioned. It is conceptually a piece of a large house. I illustrate an example in "Types of the Southern Mountain Cabin," in Brunvand, *Study of American Folklore*, p. 382(7A). Both are English forms from Virginia—the early one pre-Georgian, the later one Georgianized—and both are distinct from the more oblong Irish cabin,

for which see my little paper "Irish," in Dell Upton, ed., *America's Architectural Roots: Ethnic Groups That Built America* (Washington: National Trust for Historic Preservation, 1986), pp. 74–79. An example of two-thirds of an I-house that was filled in to complete the form can be found in *Folk Housing in Middle Virginia*, p. 92. The segmentable central-chimney house of the North can be seen in Ernest Allen Connolly's "The Cape Cod House: An Introduction," *Journal of the Society of Architectural Historians* 19:2 (1960): 47–56.

Pp. 129–30. *The Guernsey Farmhouse: A Survey by Members of the Guernsey Society* (St. Peter Port: Toucan Press, 1978) shows clearly the older (hall-and-parlor) and the newer (I-house) forms, but unfortunately it does not picture the fractional forms. Since scholarly values differ, since what is too new to be interesting to historians in one place might be crucial to historians in another, there is no substitute for fieldwork in comparative study.

P. 130. The German house of Pennsylvania typically has a central chimney and a three-room plan that is not amenable to segmentation in the manner of American Georgian houses. Instead, it was built in large and small versions of the whole form. See: Robert C. Bucher, "The Continental Log House," *Pennsylvania Folklife* 12:4 (1962): 14–19; Henry Glassie, "A Central Chimney Continental Log House," *Pennsylvania Folklife* 18:2 (1968–1969): 32–39; Scott T. Swank, *Arts of the Pennsylvania Germans* (New York: W.W. Norton for Winterthur, 1983), pp. 26–34; and Philip E. Pendleton, *Oley Valley Heritage: The Colonial Years, 1700–1775* (Birdsboro: Pennsylvania German Society, 1994), pp. 57–58, 70–73. Edward C. Chappell excellently documented houses that expressed the German form and houses that synthesized German and British ideas in the Valley of Virginia in "Acculturation in the Shenandoah Valley: Rhenish Houses of the Massanutten Settlement," *Transactions of the American Philosophical Society* 124:1 (1980): 55–89, reprinted in Upton and Vlach, *Common Places,* pp. 27–57. The usual Pennsylvania-German compromise was a house with the old plan and a regularized facade with two front doors; see my paper in *Common Places,* pp. 406–8. Though it looked symmetrical, the facade was usually only approximately so, and the plan was not symmetrical, so even when Georgianized, the German house did not fit into the symmetrical, segmentable system.

Pp. 131–32. Irish farmhouses: Evans, *Irish Heritage,* chapters 7–8; Evans, *Irish Folk Ways,* chapters 4–5; Kevin Danaher, *The Pleasant Land of Ireland* (Cork: Mercier Press, 1970), chapter 2; Kevin Danaher, *Ireland's Vernacular Architecture* (Cork: Mercier Press for The Cultural Relations Committee of Ireland, 1975); and Timothy P. O'Neill, *Life and Tradition in Rural Ireland* (London: J. M. Dent, 1977), chapter 1. Now the best book is Alan Gailey, *Rural Houses of the North of Ireland* (Edinburgh: John Donald, 1984); see especially chapter 8. I tell the story of change in *Passing the Time in Ballymenone,* pp. 376–424. For Georgian houses in Ireland: Hugh Dixon, *An Introduction to Ulster Architecture* (Belfast: Ulster Architectural Heritage Society, 1975), pp. 37, 39–42, 47, 50; and Maurice Craig, *Classic Irish Houses of the Middle Size* (New York: Architectural Book Publishing Company, 1977).

P. 132. Neither archaeological nor documentary research has solved the problem of dating in Middle Virginia. The best technique remains the quickest one: comparisons made on the basis of material evidence in the buildings—something I would do much better today than I did in 1966. Lacking dates for specific houses, I derived dates for architectural types from houses in the wider region. Then assigning dates to particular houses from an abstract typology, I dated many of those in my small area of study too early, but still got the regional sequence about right, so that, for example, Rhys Isaac in his fine *Transformation of Virginia* can comment in three separate footnotes (pp. 365, 370, 406) that people have told him that my dates are too early, which many are, and yet in his text he can adopt my argument without modification (pp. 72–74, 302–6, 310–12, 327, 334). I suppose that the pattern in the area I studied is much like the one Bernard L. Herman found in another area at the Chesapeake edge; see his *Architecture and Rural Life in Central Delaware, 1700–1900* (Knoxville: University of Tennessee Press, 1987). First comes the shift to more permanent materials, and the landscape is dominated by hall-and-parlor houses. The change to the I-house begins about 1750. So far, the patterns are comparable, but I clamped the period of transition between 1760 and 1810, when, as in Delaware, the hall-and-parlor house continued to be built well into the nineteenth century. The pattern is looser, the change took longer than I thought, but there were hall-and-parlor houses in the beginning (of the record as it exists in buildings), and there were I-houses at the end, and the change from one to the other started before the Revolution.

P. 135. Billy Price and the band: Glassie, *Passing the Time in Ballymenone,* pp. 272–79, 400.

P. 136. As Raymond Williams argues in *The Country and the City* (Oxford: Oxford University Press, 1973), especially chapter 10, people always look backward to a time when community was stronger. Nostalgia seems a permanent state of affairs. But E. P. Thompson, in *Making History: Writings on History and Culture* (New York: The New Press, 1994), pp. 245–47, counters that something really did change with enclosure, and Thompson supports his case by documenting resistance in *Customs in Common* (New York: The New Press, 1991) chapters 3–4. Thompson, I believe, is right. People seem always to lament the decline in community as part of an argument for preserving community in the future. Since they do, their words do not help us see the big change when it happens. We become trapped in an oscillation between progressive and reactionary rhetorics, and we try to make sense of them, not by studying communities at first hand, but by extrapolating from our little circles of friendship to concoct a dream of a compact, harmonious social entity in the past. Then always finding conflict in the record, we always think community is on the wane. Signs of conflict caused Michael Wood to date the decline of the village to the fourteenth century in *Domesday: A Search for the Roots of England* (New York: Facts on File, 1986), pp. 197–98. But it is not the absence of conflict that signals the presence of community. Conflict is the negative side of the engagement that keeps community alive. All communities are about to break apart. They are held together by volitional conduct, by the constant engagement that results, not from mere friendship, but from a concept of interlinked destiny. Documents, as E. P. Thompson argues in *Customs in Common,* chapter 2, tell us only the views of a privileged few who might be progressive, reactionary, or both. Conflict and longing for the past are part of the continuity of human life. But that does not mean that community is a dream and change a delusion. Material culture tells us exactly when, in the course of time through a particular landscape, engagement, and therefore community, ceases to be a high priority. It is when land and dwelling both become private: when a closed house stands on an enclosed landscape. New England had closed houses in the seventeenth century when Virginia had an enclosed landscape. Then both developed the full modern combination between, say, 1750 and 1840, as Ballymenone did in the twentieth century. The full change happened as early as the sixteenth century in southern England. In much of the world, it has not yet happened and may never happen.

P. 137. See Cary Carson, Norman F. Barka, William M. Kelso, Gary Wheeler Stone, and Dell Upton, "Impermanent Architecture in the Southern Colonies," *Winterthur Portfolio* 16:2/3 (1981): 135–96. James Deetz interprets these important findings in *Flowerdew Hundred,* pp. 53–54, 73–76; and *In Small Things Forgotten,* p. 33.

P. 138. See: Eric Mercer, *English Vernacular Houses,* pp. 1–9, 28–37, 59–62, 74–75; W. G. Hoskins, *Making of the English Landscape,* pp. 119–24; and Hoskins, *Provincial England,* chapter 7; and see these excellent books by M. W. Barley: *The English Farmhouse and Cottage,* pp. 45–47, 123–25;

and *The House and Home* (Greenwich: New York Graphic Society, 1963), pp. 18–26, 40–42.

Pp. 138–40. Upton, *Architecture in the United States,* p. 12. The best treatment we have of the architecture of a single state is Catherine Bishir's *North Carolina Architecture* (Chapel Hill: University of North Carolina Press for The Historic Preservation Foundation of North Carolina, 1990). In it, she surprisingly, accurately, and laudably ends her consideration of the nineteenth century by describing the plain and traditional buildings that are so often neglected in progressive narratives (pp. 287–309). Comparably, in taking up the national task, Peter Ennals and Deryck W. Holdsworth usefully and correctly balance the historical narrative with a chapter on "The Enduring Folk Stream" in part 2, dealing with the era of industrial capitalism, in their fine book *Homeplace: The Making of the Canadian Dwelling Over Three Centuries* (Toronto: University of Toronto Press, 1998).

P. 141. Chris Wilson, "When a Room Is the Hall: The Houses of West Las Vegas, New Mexico," in Carter, *Images of an American Land,* pp. 121–23.

P. 141. The best description of a single house ever written is James Agee's account of the dogtrot house in *Let Us Now Praise Famous Men* (Boston: Houghton Mifflin, 1960, pub. 1941), pp. 134–89. Examples of dogtrot houses: Eugene M. Wilson, *Alabama Folk Houses* (Montgomery: Alabama Historical Commission, 1975), pp. 30, 32–39; Howard Wight Marshall, *Folk Architecture in Little Dixie* (Columbia: University of Missouri Press,

1981), pp. 52–57; and Jean Sizemore, *Ozark Vernacular Houses: A Study of Rural Homeplaces in the Arkansas Ozarks, 1830–1930* (Fayetteville: University of Arkansas Press, 1994), pp. 63–73.

Pp. 141–42. Examples of these houses with two front doors: Glassie, *Pattern in the Material Folk Culture of the Eastern United States,* pp. 57–59, 82–83, 103–6, 140–41. The houses of Louisiana are ably presented by Jay D. Edwards in *Louisiana's Remarkable French Vernacular Architecture: 1700–1900* (Baton Rouge: L.S.U. Department of Geography and Anthropology, 1988). For Pennsylvania, see the note to p. 130 above.

P. 143. Native American examples: Peter Nabokov, *Architecture of Acoma Pueblo: The 1934 Historic American Buildings Survey Project* (Santa Fe: Ancient City Press, 1986); Stephen C. Jett and Virginia E. Spencer, *Navajo Architecture* (Tucson: University of Arizona Press, 1981). Hispanic houses of the Southwest: Bainbridge Bunting, *Early Architecture in New Mexico* (Albuquerque: University of New Mexico Press, 1976), chapter 3; Bainbridge Bunting, *Taos Adobes* (Santa Fe: Museum of New Mexico Press, 1964); and Chris Wilson and David Kammer, *La Tierra Amarilla: Its History, Architecture, and Cultural Landscape* (Santa Fe: Museum of New Mexico Press, 1989), chapter 2. Chris Wilson summaries the Hispanic tradition efficiently in *The Myth of Santa Fe* (Albuquerque: University of New Mexico Press, 1997), pp. 34–39. The shotgun house: John Michael Vlach, "The Shotgun House: An African Architectural Legacy," in Upton and Vlach, *Common Places,* pp. 58–78; and Philippe Oszuscik, "African-Americans in the American

South," in Allen G. Noble, ed., *To Build in a New Land* (Baltimore: Johns Hopkins University Press, 1992), pp. 157–76.

Pp. 146–48. Examples: Alec Clifton-Taylor, *English Parish Churches as Works of Art* (London: B. T. Batsford, 1974); Roar Hauglid, *Norwegische Stabkirchen* (Oslo: Dreyers Forlag, 1970); Jean-Paul Bourdier and Trinh T. Minh-ha, *Drawn from African Dwellings* (Bloomington: Indiana University Press, 1996), chapter 6; and Henri Stierlin, *Hindu India: From Khajuraho to the Temple City of Madurai* (Cologne: Taschen, 1998).

P. 148. Beware histories that begin at the beginning. Time is segmented, given a narrative order with a beginning and an end, only by a historian with a particular interest to explore and case to make. I exemplify historical research as I think it should be practiced (in the Sartrean manner), when I start in the middle of time, at the architectural change in Virginia, and then move backward and forward at once to develop and refine an explanation. Here, playing with historical convention, I assert a beginning at about the year 1000, after the Anglo-Saxons had made the lowlands of Britain into a place of openfield villages, and before their descendants dismantled their creation through enclosure.

P. 148. The attitudes and practices that power modern capitalism were sins and crimes before the Reformation; see R. H. Tawney, *Religion and the Rise of Capitalism* (London: Penguin, 1990, pub. 1926), pp. 43–67, 145–46, 184–85, 232–51. And see Matthew 19:24.

P. 149. Here is the problem. When historians restrict their understanding to the written record, there is no alternative to viewing cultural change as the creation of a literate elite. Intellectuals develop ideologies that politicians then formulate into policies that men of power, commanders of armies and leaders of business, then enact to create the world in which the common people adjust and endure. But the record of material culture suggests repetitively that people at common work create new patterns that intellectuals subsequently struggle to articulate, that politicians do not invent but belatedly ratify in policy. In his relentlessly brilliant book *The Rites of Assent: Transformations in the Symbolic Construction of America* (New York: Routledge, 1993), chapter 9, Sacvan Bercovitch describes Ralph Waldo Emerson formulating an American ideology in 1842. Emerson imagined the nation as a unity of isolated individuals, each acting honorably. That nation had been created before Emerson's birth, when American workers built closed, symmetrical houses and set them in isolation on a landscape divided by enclosure.

P. 152. An ivory figurine from India, found at Pompeii: Vidya Dehejia, *Indian Art* (London: Phaidon, 1997), p. 111.

P. 152. Mihaly Csikszentmihalyi and Eugene Rochberg-Halton have written excellently on how people attach meanings to possessions in *The Meaning of Things: Domestic Symbols and the Self* (Cambridge: Cambridge University Press, 1981). The topic that remains is how people create anew by altering and arranging possessions. In architecture, the topic divides. One part is exterior decoration, and Richard Westmacott has written a fine book on *African-American Gardens and Yards in* *the Rural South* (Knoxville: University of Tennessee Press, 1992). The other aspect is interior decoration, on which I have directed a few theses, the best being Shannon A. Docherty's "Home Decorating: Contemporary American Folk Art," Ph.D. in Folklore (Bloomington: Indiana University, May 1994). In it, through patient description of real houses, she isolated some of the important patterns in twentieth-century practice.

Pp. 154. In his critical essay on contemporary practice, *Inside Architecture* (Cambridge: The MIT Press, 1996), p. 53, Vittorio Gregotti writes that building is no longer a matter of giving form to materials but of arranging manufactured products.

Pp. 154–57. I describe the change in western Anatolia in *Turkish Traditional Art Today*, pp. 252–64. Turkey helps to clarify the argument. In Virginia, certain Georgian features—hallways and symmetrical facades—began to be adopted generally soon after they were introduced (even if it took a century to complete the Georgianizing process), so it is not obvious that elements of the new style were adopted, not merely because they were new, but because they were socially useful. (Had sheer newness been the goal, Virginians would have accepted the whole Georgian package. Were fashion a sufficient explanation, they would have continued to adopt new forms through the nineteenth century when they continued to build I-houses.) In Ireland, the Georgian form was also introduced in the eighteenth century, but it was not generally adopted until the twentieth, showing clearly that conditions had to develop to the point where people wanted what the style had to offer. In Turkey, houses with central hallways for circulation are an old part of the tradition, quite general by the eighteenth century, but the village people of the northern Aegean did not begin borrowing the idea until the 1960s. To note a change in fashion makes a beginning, but what we must learn from formal analysis is exactly what changed (realizing that change is always accompanied by continuity), and what we must learn from contextual analysis is why there is, in a particular historical moment, a particular mix of change and continuity.

180

BIBLIOGRAPHY

Aalen, F. H. A. *Man and the Landscape in Ireland*. London: Academic Press, 1978.

Aalen, F. H. A., Kevin Whelan, and Matthew Stout, eds. *Atlas of the Irish Rural Landscape*. Cork: Cork University Press, 1997.

Addy, Sidney Oldall. *The Evolution of the English House*. London: Swan Sonnenschein, 1898.

Agee, James, and Walker Evans. *Let Us Now Praise Famous Men*. Boston: Houghton Mifflin, 1960 [1941].

Armstrong, Robert Plant. *The Affecting Presence: An Essay in Humanistic Anthropology*. Urbana: University of Illinois Press, 1971.

———. *Wellspring: On the Myth and Source of Culture*. Berkeley: University of California Press, 1975.

———. *The Powers of Presence: Consciousness, Myth, and Affecting Presence*. Philadelphia: University of Pennsylvania Press, 1981.

Arnold, Dana, ed. *The Georgian Villa*. Phoenix Mill: Alan Sutton, 1996.

A:son-Palmqvist, Lena. *Building Traditions among Swedish Settlers in Rural Minnesota: Material Culture—Reflecting Persistence or Decline of Traditions*. Stockholm: Nordiska Museet, 1983.

Attebery, Jennifer Eastman. *Building Idaho: An Architectural History*. Moscow: University of Idaho Press, 1991.

———. *Building with Logs: Western Log Construction in Context*. Moscow: University of Idaho Press, 1998.

Ayres, James. *The Shell Book of the Home in Britain: Decoration, Design and Construction of Vernacular Interiors, 1500–*
1850. London: Faber and Faber, 1981.

———. *Building the Georgian City*. New Haven: Yale University Press, 1998.

Bachelard, Gaston. *The Poetics of Space*. Trans. Maria Jolas. Boston: Beacon Press, 1969 [1958].

Bahloul, Joëlle. *The Architecture of Memory: A Jewish-Muslim Household in Colonial Algeria, 1937–1962*. Cambridge: Cambridge University Press, 1996 [1992].

Barley, M. W. *The English Farmhouse and Cottage*. London: Routledge and Kegan Paul, 1961.

———. *The House and Home: A Review of 900 Years of House Planning and Furnishing in Britain*. Greenwich: New York Graphic Society, 1971.

Baxandall, Michael. *Patterns of Intention: On the Historical Explanation of Pictures*. New Haven: Yale University Press, 1985.

Benes, Peter, and Phillip D. Zimmerman. *New England Meeting House and Church: 1630–1850*. Dublin: Dublin Seminar for New England Folklife, 1979.

Bercovitch, Sacvan. *The Puritan Origins of the American Self*. New Haven: Yale University Press, 1975.

———. *The Rites of Assent: Transformations in the Symbolic Construction of America*. New York: Routledge, 1994.

Bishir, Catherine W. *North Carolina Architecture*. Chapel Hill: University of North Carolina Press for The Historic Preservation Foundation of North Carolina, 1990.

Bloch, Marc. *The Historian's Craft*. Trans.

Peter Putnam. New York: Vintage Books, 1953.

———. *Land and Work in Mediaeval Europe*. Trans. J. E. Anderson. New York: Harper and Row, 1969.

———. *Feudal Society*. Trans. L. A. Manyon. 2 vols. Chicago: University of Chicago Press, 1964.

Bluestone, Daniel. *Constructing Chicago*. New Haven: Yale University Press, 1991.

Boas, Franz. *Primitive Art*. New York: Dover, 1955 [1927].

Bourdier, Jean-Paul, and Nezar AlSayyad, eds. *Dwellings, Settlements, and Traditions: Cross-Cultural Perspectives*. Lanham: University Press of America, 1989.

Bourdier, Jean-Paul, and Trinh T. Minh-ha. *African Spaces: Designs for Living in Upper Volta*. New York: Africana, 1985.

———. *Drawn from African Dwellings*. Bloomington: Indiana University Press, 1996.

Bowe, Nicola Gordon, ed. *Art and the National Dream: The Search for Vernacular Expression in Turn-of- the-Century Design*. Dublin: Irish Academic Press, 1993.

Branch, Daniel Paulk. *Folk Architecture of the Eastern Mediterranean*. New York: Columbia University Press, 1966.

Brand, Stewart. *How Buildings Learn: What Happens After They're Built*. New York: Penguin, 1994.

Braudel, Fernand. *The Mediterranean and the Mediterranean World in the Age of Philip II*. Trans. Sián Reynolds. 2 vols. New York: Harper and Row, 1972.

———. *On History*. Trans. Sarah Matthews. Chicago: University of Chicago Press, 1980.

Brinkman, Marilyn Salzi, and William Towner Morgan. *Light from the Hearth: Central Minnesota Pioneers and Early Architecture*. Saint Cloud: North Star Press, 1982.

Brunskill, R. W. *Illustrated Handbook of Vernacular Architecture*. New York: Universe Books, 1970.

———. *Vernacular Architecture of the Lake Counties: A Field Handbook*. London: Faber and Faber, 1974.

———. *Houses*. London: Collins, 1982.

———. *Traditional Farm Buildings of Britain*. London: Victor Gollancz, 1982.

Bunting, Bainbridge. *Taos Adobes: Spanish Colonial and Territorial Architecture in the Taos Valley*. Santa Fe: Museum of New Mexico Press, 1964.

———. *Early Architecture in New Mexico*. Albuquerque: University of New Mexico Press, 1976.

Bunzel, Ruth L. *The Pueblo Potter: A Study of Creative Imagination in Primitive Art*. New York: Dover, 1972 [1929].

Burcaw, George Ellis. *The Saxon House: A Cultural Index in European Ethnography*. Moscow: University Press of Idaho, 1979.

Burckhardt, Titus. *Art of Islam: Language and Meaning*. Westerham: World of Islam Festival, 1976.

Burke, Peter. *Popular Culture in Early Modern Europe*. Aldershot: Wildwood House, 1988 [1978].

Butterfield, Herbert. *The Whig Interpretation of History*. New York: W.W. Norton, 1965.

Caffyn, Lucy. *Workers' Housing in West Yorkshire, 1750–1920*. London: Royal Commission on the Historical Monuments of England, 1986.

Carney, George O., ed. *Baseball, Barns,*

and Bluegrass: A Geography of American Folklife. Lanham: Rowman and Littlefield, 1998.

Carter, Thomas, ed. *Images of an American Land: Vernacular Architecture in the Western United States*. Albuquerque: University of New Mexico Press, 1997.

Carter, Thomas, and Blanton Owen. *Designed for Work: The San Jacinto Ranch of Elko County, Nevada*. Salt Lake City: Graduate School of Architecture, University of Utah, 1993.

Carver, Norman F., Jr. *Japanese Folkhouses*. Kalamazoo: Documan Press, 1984.

Chang, K. C., ed. *Settlement Archaeology*. Palo Alto: National Press Books, 1968.

Chinnery, Victor. *Oak Furniture in the British Tradition: A History of Early Furniture in the British Isles and New England*. Woodbridge: Antique Collectors' Club, 1979.

Comeaux, Malcolm. *Atchafalaya Swamp Life: Settlement and Folk Occupations*. Baton Rouge: Geoscience and Man, 1972.

Coomaraswamy, Ananda K. *The Transformation of Nature in Art*. Cambridge: Harvard University Press, 1935.

Cooper, Ilay, and Barry Dawson. *Traditional Buildings of India*. London: Thames and Hudson, 1998.

Csikszentmihalyi, Mihaly, and Eugene Rochberg-Halton. *The Meaning of Things: Domestic Symbols and the Self*. Cambridge: Cambridge University Press, 1985.

Cummings, Abbott Lowell. *The Framed Houses of Massachusetts Bay, 1625–1725*. Cambridge: Harvard University Press, 1979.

Deetz, James. *Invitation to Archaeology*. Garden City: Natural History Press, 1967.

———. *Flowerdew Hundred: The Archaeology of a Virginia Plantation, 1619–1864*. Charlottesville: University Press of Virginia, 1993.

———. *In Small Things Forgotten: An Archaeology of Early American Life*. New York: Anchor Books, 1996 [1977].

Dornbusch, Charles H., and John K. Heyl. *Pennsylvania German Barns*. Allentown: Schlechter's for the Pennsylvania German Folklore Society, 1958.

Eames, Penelope. *Furniture in England, France and the Netherlands from the Twelfth to the Fifteenth Century*. London: Furniture History Society, 1977.

Engel, Heinrich. *The Japanese House: A Tradition for Contemporary Architecture*. Rutland: Charles E. Tuttle, 1988 [1964].

Ennals, Peter, and Deryck W. Holdsworth. *Homeplace: The Making of the Canadian Dwelling over Three Centuries*. Toronto: University of Toronto Press, 1998.

Ensminger, Robert F. *The Pennsylvania Barn: Its Origin, Evolution, and Distribution in North America*. Baltimore: Johns Hopkins University Press, 1992.

Evans, E. Estyn. *Irish Folk Ways*. New York: Devin-Adair, 1957.

———. *Mourne Country: Landscape and Life in South Down*. Dundalk: Dundalgan Press, 1967.

———. *The Personality of Ireland: Habitat, Heritage and History*. Cambridge: University Press, 1973.

———. *Ireland and the Atlantic Heritage*. Dublin: Lilliput Press, 1996.

Fairbanks, Jonathan L., and Robert F. Trent, eds. *New England Begins: The*

Seventeenth Century. 3 vols. Boston: Museum of Fine Arts, 1982.

Fenton, Alexander. The Northern Isles: Orkney and Shetland. Edinburgh: John Donald, 1978.

Fenton, Alexander, and Bruce Walker. The Rural Architecture of Scotland. Edinburgh: John Donald, 1981.

Ferguson, Leland, ed. Historical Archaeology and the Importance of Material Things. Columbia: Society for Historical Archaeology, 1977.

Fischer, David Hackett. Albion's Seed: Four British Folkways in America. New York: Oxford University Press, 1989.

Fitch, James Marston. American Building 2: The Environmental Forces That Shape It. Boston: Houghton Mifflin, 1972.

———. Historic Preservation: Curatorial Management of the Built World. New York: McGraw-Hill, 1982.

Fitch, James Marston, and William Bobenhausen. American Building: The Environmental Forces That Shape It. New York: Oxford University Press, 1999.

Fitchen, John. The New World Dutch Barn: A Study of Its Characteristics, Its Structural System, and Its Probable Erection Procedures. Syracuse: Syracuse University Press, 1968.

Forman, Henry Chandlee. The Architecture of the Old South: The Medieval Style, 1585–1850. Cambridge: Harvard University Press, 1948.

———. Tidewater Maryland Architecture and Gardens. New York: Bonanza, 1956.

Forrester, Harry. The Timber-Framed Houses of Essex: A Short Survey of their Types and Details, 14th to 18th Centuries. Chelmsford: Tindal Press, 1965.

Fox, Sir Cyril. The Personality of Britain: Its Influence on Inhabitant and Invader in Prehistoric and Early Historic Times. Cardiff: National Museum of Wales, 1952 [1932].

Fox, Sir Cyril, and Lord Raglan. Monmouthshire Houses: A Study of Building Techniques and Smaller House-Plans in the Fifteenth to Seventeenth Centuries. 3 vols. Cardiff: National Museum of Wales, 1951–1954.

Frescura, Franco. Rural Shelter in Southern Africa: A Survey of the Architecture, House Forms and Construction Methods of the Black Rural Peoples of Southern Africa. Johannesburg: Ravan Press, 1981.

Fryer, Judith. Felicitous Space: The Imaginative Structures of Edith Wharton and Willa Cather. Chapel Hill: University of North Carolina Press, 1986.

Frykman, Jonas, and Orvar Löfgren. Culture Builders: A Historical Anthropology of Middle-Class Life. Trans. Alan Crozier. New Brunswick: Rutgers University Press, 1987.

Gailey, Alan. Rural Houses of the North of Ireland. Edinburgh: John Donald, 1984.

Garrison, J. Ritchie. Landscape and Material Life in Franklin County, Massachusetts, 1770–1860. Knoxville: University of Tennessee Press, 1991.

Garvan, Anthony N. B. Architecture and Town Planning in Colonial Connecticut. New Haven: Yale University Press, 1951.

Gillis, John R. A World of Their Own Making: Myth, Ritual, and the Quest for Family Values. New York: Basic Books, 1996.

Glassie, Henry. Pattern in the Material Folk Culture of the Eastern United States. Philadelphia: University of Pennsylvania Press, 1968.

———. *Folk Housing in Middle Virginia: A Structural Analysis of Historic Artifacts*. Knoxville: University of Tennessee Press, 1975.

———. *Passing the Time in Ballymenone: Culture and History of an Ulster Community*. Philadelphia: University of Pennsylvania Press, 1982.

———. *The Spirit of Folk Art*. New York: Abrams and Museum of International Folk Art, 1989.

———. *Turkish Traditional Art Today*. Bloomington: Indiana University Press, 1993.

———. *Art and Life in Bangladesh*. Bloomington: Indiana University Press, 1997.

———. *Material Culture*. Bloomington: Indiana University Press, 1999.

Goldstein, Kenneth S. *A Guide for Field Workers in Folklore*. Hatboro: Folklore Associates, 1964.

Goodwin, Godfrey. *A History of Ottoman Architecture*. London: Thames and Hudson, 1971.

Gowans, Alan. *Images of American Living: Four Centuries of Architecture and Furniture as Cultural Expression*. Philadelphia: J. B. Lippincott, 1964.

Gregotti, Vittorio. *Inside Architecture*. Trans. Peter Wong and Francesca Zaccheo. Cambridge: The MIT Press, 1996.

Griffith, James S. *Beliefs and Holy Places: A Spiritual Geography of the Pimeria Alta*. Tucson: University of Arizona Press, 1992.

Gudmundson, Wayne, and Suzanne Winckler. *Testaments in Wood: Finnish Log Structures at Embarrass, Minnesota*. St. Paul: Minnesota Historical Society Press, 1991.

Günay, Reha. *Tradition of the Turkish House and Safranbolu Houses*. Trans. Çelen Birkan. Istanbul: YEM Yayın, 1998.

Hart, John Fraser. *The Rural Landscape*. Baltimore: Johns Hopkins University Press, 1998.

Heimsath, Clovis. *Pioneer Texas Buildings: A Geometry Lesson*. Austin: University of Texas Press, 1968.

Herman, Bernard L. *Architecture and Rural Life in Central Delaware, 1700–1900*. Knoxville: University of Tennessee Press, 1987.

———. *The Stolen House*. Charlottesville: University Press of Virginia, 1992.

Hewett, Cecil Alec. *The Development of Carpentry, 1200–1700: An Essex Study*. Newton Abbot: David and Charles, 1969.

Hill, Christopher. *Change and Continuity in Seventeenth-Century England*. Cambridge: Harvard University Press, 1975.

Hoskins, W.G. *The Making of the English Landscape*. London: Hodder and Stoughton, 1955.

———. *The Midland Peasant: The Economic and Social History of a Leicestershire Village*. London: Macmillan, 1965.

———. *Provincial England: Essays in Social and Economic History*. London: Macmillan, 1965.

———. *Fieldwork in Local History*. London: Faber and Faber, 1969.

Hubka, Thomas C. *Big House, Little House, Back House, Barn: The Connected Farm Buildings of New England*. Hanover: University Press of New England, 1984.

Hunt, Marjorie. *The Stone Carvers: Master Craftsmen of Washington National Cathedral*. Washington: Smithsonian Institution Press, 1999.

Hutslar, Donald A. *Log Construction in the Ohio Country, 1750–1850*. Athens: Ohio University Press, 1992.

Hymes, Dell, ed. *Reinventing Anthropology*. New York: Pantheon, 1972.

Ingersoll, Daniel W., Jr., and Gordon Bronitsky, eds. *Mirror and Metaphor: Material and Social Constructions of Reality*. Lanham: University Press of America, 1987.

Innocent, C. F. *The Development of English Building Construction*. Newton Abbot: David and Charles, 1971 [1916].

Isaac, Rhys. *The Transformation of Virginia: 1740–1780*. New York: W. W. Norton, 1988 [1982].

Itoh, Teiji. *Traditional Domestic Architecture of Japan*. Trans. Richard L. Gage. New York: Weatherhill/Heibonsha, 1979.

——— . *The Gardens of Japan*. Tokyo: Kodansha, 1998 [1984].

Jackson, John Brinckerhoff. *Discovering the Vernacular Landscape*. New Haven: Yale University Press, 1984.

Jakle, John A., Robert W. Bastian, and Douglas K. Meyer. *Common Houses in America's Small Towns*. Athens: University of Georgia Press, 1989.

James, John. *Chartres: The Masons Who Built a Legend*. London: Routledge and Kegan Paul, 1985.

Jett, Stephen C., and Virginia E. Spencer. *Navajo Architecture: Forms, History, Distributions*. Tucson: University of Arizona Press, 1981.

Johnson, Matthew. *Housing Culture: Traditional Architecture in an English Landscape*. London: UCL Press, 1993.

Jones, Michael Owen. *Craftsman of the Cumberlands: Tradition and Creativity*. Lexington: University Press of Kentucky, 1989 [1975].

Jordan, Terry G. *Texas Log Buildings: A Folk Architecture*. Austin: University of Texas Press, 1978.

Joyner, Charles. *Down by the Riverside: A South Carolina Slave Community*. Urbana: University of Illinois Press, 1984.

——— . *Shared Traditions: Southern History and Folk Culture*. Urbana: University of Illinois Press, 1999.

Kelly, J. Frederick. *The Early Domestic Architecture of Connecticut*. New Haven: Yale University Press, 1924.

Kirk, John T. *American Furniture and the British Tradition to 1830*. New York: Alfred A. Knopf, 1982.

Kirker, Harold. *California's Architectural Frontier: Style and Tradition in the Nineteenth Century*. Santa Barbara: Peregrine Smith, 1973.

Klein, Barbro, and Mats Widbom, eds. *Swedish Folk Art: All Tradition Is Change*. New York: Abrams, 1994.

Knapp, Ronald G. *China's Traditional Rural Architecture: A Cultural Geography of the Common House*. Honolulu: University of Hawaii Press, 1986.

Koop, Michael, and Stephen Ludwig. *German-Russian Folk Architecture in Southeastern South Dakota*. Vermillion: State Historical Preservation Center, 1984.

Kostof, Spiro. *Caves of God: The Monastic Environment of Byzantine Cappadocia*. Cambridge: The MIT Press, 1972.

Kramrisch, Stella. *The Hindu Temple*. 2 vols. Delhi: Motilal Banarsidass, 1996 [1946].

Kubler, George. *The Shape of Time: Remarks on the History of Things*. New Haven: Yale University Press, 1962.

——— . *The Religious Architecture of New*

Mexico in the Colonial Period and Since the American Occupation. Albuquerque: University of New Mexico Press for the School of American Research, 1972.

Küçükerman, Önder. *Turkish House: In Search of Spatial Identity.* Istanbul: Turkish Touring and Automobile Association, 1985.

Kuban, Doğan. *The Turkish Hayat House.* Istanbul: Eren, 1995.

Kuran, Aptullah. *The Mosque in Early Ottoman Architecture.* Chicago: University of Chicago Press, 1968.

———. *Sinan: The Grand Old Master of Ottoman Architecture.* Washington: Institute of Turkish Studies, 1987.

Lanier, Gabrielle M., and Bernard L. Herman. *Everyday Architecture of the Mid-Atlantic: Looking at Buildings and Landscapes.* Baltimore: Johns Hopkins University Press, 1997.

Larkin, Jack. *The Reshaping of Everyday Life, 1790–1840.* New York: Harper and Row, 1988.

Le Corbusier. *Towards a New Architecture.* London: Architectural Press, 1952 [1927].

———. *When the Cathedrals Were White.* New York: McGraw-Hill, 1964 [1947].

———. *Journey to the East.* Trans. and ed. Ivan Zaknić. Cambridge: The MIT Press, 1989 [1966].

Leone, Mark P., and Parker B. Potter, Jr. *The Recovery of Meaning: Historical Archaeology in the Eastern United States.* Washington: Smithsonian Institution Press, 1988.

Lévi-Strauss, Claude. *The Savage Mind.* Chicago: University of Chicago Press, 1966.

———. *The Way of the Masks.* Trans. Sylvia Modelski. Seattle: University of Washington Press, 1982.

Long, Amos, Jr. *The Pennsylvania German Family Farm.* Breinigsville: The Pennsylvania German Society, 1972.

Macfarlane, Alan. *Reconstructing Historical Communities.* Cambridge: Cambridge University Press, 1977.

Mahmud, Firoz. *Prospects of Material Folk Culture Studies and Folklife Museums in Bangladesh.* Dhaka: Bangla Academy, 1993.

Mango, Cyril. *Byzantine Architecture.* New York: Abrams, 1974.

Marshall, Howard Wight. *Folk Architecture in Little Dixie: A Regional Culture in Missouri.* Columbia: University of Missouri Press, 1981.

———. *Paradise Valley, Nevada: The People and Buildings of an American Place.* Tucson: University of Arizona Press, 1995.

Martin, Charles E. *Hollybush: Folk Building and Social Change in an Appalachian Community.* Knoxville: University of Tennessee Press, 1984.

Megas, George A. *The Greek House: Its Evolution and Its Relation to the Houses of the Other Balkan Peoples.* Athens: Ministry of Reconstruction, 1951.

Meinig, D. W., ed. *The Interpretation of Ordinary Landscapes.* Oxford: Oxford University Press, 1979.

———. *The Shaping of America: A Geographical Perspective on 500 Years of History: I: Atlantic America, 1492–1800.* New Haven: Yale University Press, 1986.

Meirion-Jones, Gwyn I. *The Vernacular Architecture of Brittany: An Essay in Historical Geography.* Edinburgh: John Donald, 1982.

Mercer, Eric. *Furniture, 700–1700.* New York: Meredith Press, 1969.

———. *English Vernacular Houses: A*

Study of Traditional Farmhouses and Cottages. London: Royal Commission on Historical Monuments, 1975.

Mercer, Henry C. *Ancient Carpenters' Tools.* Doylestown: Bucks County Historical Society, 1960 [1929].

Michell, George. *The Hindu Temple: An Introduction to Its Meaning and Forms.* Chicago: University of Chicago Press, 1988 [1977].

Moffett, Marian, and Lawrence Wodehouse. *East Tennessee Cantilever Barns.* Knoxville: University of Tennessee Press, 1993.

Moholy-Nagy, Sibyl. *Native Genius in Anonymous Architecture.* New York: Horizon Press, 1957.

Montell, William Lynwood, and Michael Lynn Morse. *Kentucky Folk Architecture.* Lexington: University Press of Kentucky, 1976.

Morris, Richard. *Churches in the Landscape.* London: Phoenix, 1997 [1989].

Morris, William. *Hopes and Fears for Art.* London: Ellis and White, 1882.

———. *Signs of Change.* London: Reeves and Turner, 1888.

———. *Architecture, Industry and Wealth: Collected Papers.* London: Longmans, Green, 1902.

Moughtin, J. C. *Hausa Architecture.* London: Ethnographica, 1985.

Murray-Wooley, Carolyn, and Karl Raitz. *Rock Fences of the Bluegrass.* Lexington: University Press of Kentucky, 1992.

Murtagh, William J. *Moravian Architecture and Town Planning: Bethlehem, Pennsylvania, and Other Eighteenth-Century American Settlements.* Chapel Hill: University of North Carolina Press, 1967.

Muthesius, Stefan. *The English Terraced House.* New Haven: Yale University Press, 1982.

Nabokov, Peter, and Robert Easton. *Native American Architecture.* New York: Oxford University Press, 1989.

Naismith, Robert J. *Buildings of the Scottish Countryside.* London: Victor Gollancz, 1989.

Niederer, Frances J. *The Town of Fincastle Virginia.* Charlottesville: University Press of Virginia, 1965.

Nelson, Lowry. *The Mormon Village: A Pattern and Technique of Land Settlement.* Salt Lake City: University of Utah Press, 1952.

Nelson, Marion John. *Material Culture and People's Art Among the Norwegians in America.* Northfield: Norwegian-American Historical Association, 1994.

Noble, Allen G., ed. *To Build in a New Land: Ethnic Landscapes in North America.* Baltimore: Johns Hopkins University Press, 1992.

Noble, Allen G., and Hubert G. H. Wilhelm, eds. *Barns of the Midwest.* Athens: Ohio University Press, 1995.

Norberg-Schulz, Christian. *Intentions in Architecture.* Cambridge: The MIT Press, 1965.

———. *Existence, Space and Architecture.* New York: Praeger, 1971.

———. *Genius Loci: Towards a Phenomenology of Architecture.* New York: Rizzoli, 1984.

———. *Architecture: Meaning and Place.* New York: Rizzoli, 1988.

———. *Nightlands: Nordic Building.* Cambridge: The MIT Press, 1996.

Oliver, Paul, ed. *Shelter in Africa.* New York: Praeger, 1971.

———. ed. *Encyclopedia of Vernacular Architecture of the World.* 3 vols. Cambridge: Cambridge University Press, 1997.

Paccard, André. *Traditional Islamic Craft in Moroccan Architecture.* 2 vols. Saint-Jorioz: Éditions Atelier 74, 1980.

Panofsky, Erwin. *Gothic Architecture and Scholasticism.* New York: World, 1957.

Peate, Iorwerth C. *The Welsh House: A Study in Folk Culture.* London: The Honourable Society of Cymmrodorion, 1940.

Perrin, Richard W. E. *Historic Wisconsin Buildings: A Survey of Pioneer Architecture, 1835–1870.* Milwaukee: Milwaukee Public Museum, 1962.

Peterson, Fred W. *Homes in the Heartland: Balloon Frame Farmhouses of the Upper Midwest, 1850–1920.* Lawrence: University of Kansas Press, 1992.

————. *Building the Community, Keeping the Faith: German Catholic Vernacular Architecture in a Rural Minnesota Parish.* St. Paul: Minnesota Historical Society Press, 1998.

Pevsner, Nikolaus. *Pioneers of the Modern Movement: From William Morris to Walter Gropius.* London: Faber and Faber, 1936.

Philippides, Dimitri. *Greek Traditional Architecture.* 2 vols. Athens: "Melissa," 1983.

Pocius, Gerald. *A Place to Belong: Community Order and Everyday Space in Calvert, Newfoundland.* Athens: University of Georgia Press, 1991.

————. ed. *Living in a Material World: Canadian and American Approaches to Material Culture.* St. John's: Institute of Social and Economic Research, 1991.

Powell, Sumner Chilton. *Puritan Village: The Formation of a New England Town.* Middletown: Wesleyan University Press, 1975 [1963].

Prussin, Labelle. *Architecture in Northern Ghana: A Study of Forms and Functions.* Berkeley: University of California Press, 1969.

Quiney, Anthony. *Kent Houses: English Domestic Architecture.* Woodbridge: Antique Collectors' Club, 1993.

Ragette, Friedrich. *Architecture in Lebanon: The Lebanese House During the 18th and 19th Centuries.* Beirut: American University of Beirut, 1974.

Rapoport, Amos. *House Form and Culture.* Englewood Cliffs: Prentice-Hall, 1969.

————. *The Meaning of the Built Environment: A Nonverbal Communication Approach.* Beverly Hills: Sage, 1982.

Redfield, Robert. *The Little Community: Viewpoints for the Study of a Human Whole.* Chicago: University of Chicago Press, 1955.

Rees, Alwyn D. *Life in a Welsh Countryside.* Cardiff: University of Wales Press, 1971 [1950].

Rempel, John I. *Building with Wood and Other Aspects of Nineteenth-Century Building in Ontario.* Toronto: University of Toronto Press, 1967.

Reps, John W. *Town Planning in Frontier America.* Princeton: Princeton University Press, 1969.

Roberts, Warren E. *Viewpoints on Folklife: Looking at the Overlooked.* Ann Arbor: UMI Research Press, 1988.

————. *Log Buildings of Southern Indiana.* Bloomington: Trickster Press, 1996 [1984].

St. George, Robert Blair, ed. *Material Life in America: 1680–1860.* Boston: Northeastern University Press, 1988.

————. *Conversing by Signs: Poetics of*

Implication in Colonial New England Culture. Chapel Hill: University of North Carolina Press, 1998.

Saqqaf, Abdulaziz, ed. *The Middle East City: Ancient Traditions Confront a Modern World*. New York: Paragon House, 1987.

Sartre, Jean-Paul. *Search for a Method*. Trans. Hazel E. Barnes. New York: Alfred A. Knopf, 1963.

———. *Between Existentialism and Marxism*. Trans. John Matthews. New York: William Morrow, 1976.

Schlereth, Thomas J., ed. *Material Culture Studies in America*. Nashville: AASLH, 1982.

Shurtleff, Harold R. *The Log Cabin Myth: A Study of Early Dwellings of the English Colonies in North America*. Ed. Samuel Eliot Morison. Gloucester: Peter Smith, 1967 [1939].

Sieber, Roy. *African Furniture and Household Objects*. Bloomington: Indiana University Press, 1980.

Sizemore, Jean. *Ozark Vernacular Houses: A Study of Rural Homeplaces in the Arkansas Ozarks, 1830–1930*. Fayetteville: University of Arkansas Press, 1994.

Smith, Cyril Stanley. *A Search for Structure: Selected Essays on Science, Art, and History*. Cambridge: The MIT Press, 1982.

Smith, Peter. *Houses of the Welsh Countryside: A Study in Historical Geography*. London: Royal Commission on Ancient and Historical Monuments in Wales, 1988.

Sowden, Harry. *Australian Woolsheds*. North Melbourne: Cassell Australia, 1972.

Starr, Eileen F. *Architecture in the Cowboy State, 1849–1940*. Glendo: High Plains Press, 1992.

Stea, David, and Mete Turan. *Placemaking: Production of Built Environment in Two Cultures*. Aldershot: Avebury, 1993.

Steensberg, Axel, and Grith Lerche. *Danish Peasant Furniture*. 2 vols. Copenhagen: Arnold Busck, 1989.

Stilgoe, John R. *Common Landscape of America, 1580 to 1845*. New Haven: Yale University Press, 1982.

Stotz, Charles Morse. *The Architectural Heritage of Early Western Pennsylvania: A Record of Building before 1860*. Pittsburgh: University of Pittsburgh Press, 1966 [1936].

Swaim, Doug, ed. *Carolina Dwelling: Towards Preservation of Place: In Celebration of the North Carolina Vernacular Landscape*. Raleigh: North Carolina State University, 1978.

Swank, Scott T. *Arts of the Pennsylvania Germans*. New York: W. W. Norton for Winterthur, 1983.

Tate, W. E. *The Enclosure Movement*. New York: Walker and Company, 1967.

Taylor, Christopher. *Dorset*. London: Hodder and Stoughton, 1979.

Thompson, Deborah, ed. *Maine Forms of American Architecture*. Camden: Downeast Magazine for Colby Museum of Art, 1976.

Thompson, E. P. *Whigs and Hunters: The Origin of the Black Act*. New York: Pantheon, 1975.

———. *William Morris: Romantic to Revolutionary*. New York: Pantheon, 1977.

———. *Customs in Common*. New York: The New Press, 1991.

Thompson, Robert Farris. *Flash of the Spirit: African and Afro-American Art and Philosophy*. New York: Vintage Books, 1984.

Trent, Robert F. *Hearts and Crowns: Folk Chairs of the Connecticut Coast, 1720–1840*. New Haven: New Haven Colony Historical Society, 1977.

Tuan, Yi-fu. *Space and Place: The Perspective of Experience*. Minneapolis: University of Minnesota Press, 1977.

Turan, Mete, ed. *Vernacular Architecture: Paradigms of Environmental Response*. Aldershot: Avebury, 1990.

Ulrich, Laurel Thatcher. *A Midwife's Tale: The Life of Martha Ballard, Based on Her Diary, 1785–1812*. New York: Vintage Books, 1991.

Upton, Dell. *Holy Things and Profane: Anglican Parish Churches in Colonial Virginia*. Cambridge: The MIT Press, 1986.

——— . ed. *America's Architectural Roots: Ethnic Groups That Built America*. Washington: National Trust for Historic Preservation, 1986.

——— . *Architecture in the United States*. Oxford: Oxford University Press, 1998.

Upton, Dell, and John Michael Vlach, eds. *Common Places: Readings in American Vernacular Architecture*. Athens: University of Georgia Press, 1986.

Van Ravenswaay, Charles. *The Arts and Architecture of German Settlements in Missouri: A Survey of a Vanishing Culture*. Columbia: University of Missouri Press, 1977.

Veillette, John, and Gary White. *Early Indian Churches: Wooden Frontier Architecture in British Columbia*. Vancouver: University of British Columbia Press, 1977.

Venturi, Robert. *Complexity and Contradiction in Architecture*. New York: Museum of Modern Art, 1966.

Vlach, John Michael. *The Afro-American Tradition in Decorative Arts*. Cleveland Museum of Art, 1978.

——— . *Back of the Big House: The Architecture of Plantation Slavery*. Chapel Hill: University of North Carolina Press, 1993.

Wacker, Peter O. *The Musconetcong Valley of New Jersey: A Historical Geography*. New Brunswick: Rutgers University Press, 1968.

Walker, H. Jesse, and Randall A. Detro, eds. *Cultural Diffusion and Landscapes: Selections by Fred B. Kniffen*. Baton Rouge: Geoscience Publications, 1990.

Walker, H. J., and W. G. Haag, eds. *Man and Cultural Heritage: Papers in Honor of Fred B. Kniffen*. Baton Rouge: L. S. U. School of Geoscience, 1974.

Walton, James. *African Village*. Pretoria: J. L. Van Schaik, 1956.

Warren, John, and Ihsan Fethi. *Traditional Houses in Baghdad*. Horsham: Coach, 1982.

Wells, Camille, ed. *Perspectives in Vernacular Architecture*. Annapolis: Vernacular Architecture Forum, 1982.

——— . *Perspectives in Vernacular Architecture II*. Columbia: University of Missouri Press, 1986.

Welsch, Roger. *Sod Walls: The Story of the Nebraska Sod House*. Broken Bow: Purcells, 1968.

Wenzel, Marian. *House Decoration in Nubia*. London: Duckworth, 1972.

Westmacott, Richard. *African-American Gardens and Yards in the Rural South*. Knoxville: University of Tennessee Press, 1992.

Whiffen, Marcus. *The Eighteenth-Century Houses of Williamsburg: A Study of Architecture and Building in the Colonial*

Capital of Virginia. Williamsburg: Colonial Williamsburg Foundation, 1985 [1960].

Williams, Raymond. *The Country and the City*. New York: Oxford University Press, 1973.

Wilson, Chris. *The Myth of Santa Fe: Creating a Modern Regional Tradition*. Albuquerque: University of New Mexico Press, 1997.

Wilson, Chris, and David Kammer. *La Tierra Amarilla: Its History, Architecture, and Cultural Landscape*. Santa Fe: Museum of New Mexico Press, 1992 [1989].

Wood-Jones, Raymond B. *Traditional Domestic Architecture of the Banbury Region*. Manchester: Manchester University Press, 1963.

Wright, Gwendolyn. *Building the Dream: A Social History of Housing in America*. Cambridge: The MIT Press, 1983.

Wulff, Hans E. *The Traditional Crafts of Persia: Their Development, Technology, and Influence on Eastern and Western Civilizations*. Cambridge: The MIT Press, 1966.

Yanagi, Soetsu. *The Unknown Craftsman: A Japanese Insight into Beauty*. Ed. Bernard Leach. Tokyo: Kodansha, 1989 [1972].

Yoder, Don, and Thomas E. Graves. *Hex Signs: Pennsylvania German Barn Symbols and Their Meaning*. Mechanicsburg: Stackpole Books, 2000 [1989].

Zelinsky, Wilbur. *Exploring the Beloved Country: Geographic Forays into American Society and Culture*. Iowa City: University of Iowa Press, 1994.

INDEX

VERNACULAR ARCHITECTURE
designed by
Henry Glassie
composed by
Bruce Carpenter
published by
Material Culture
and the
Indiana University Press